LEARN SQL:

Table of Contents

Introduction

What is SQL?

Before you can begin experimenting with SQL, you must have access to a database system. There are various online SQL editors you can use to evaluate or test SQL statements I have provided as examples in this book. However, you need a full-fledged database management system in order to execute SQL statements.

Basic Terms

What is Relational Database?

A relational database is a type of database categorized into tables with each table relating to another within the database. It allows data to be divided into smaller, logical, and manageable units for better performance and easier maintenance. To relate one table to another, you need to create a common field or key in a relational database system.

Definition Data

Data is a fact that relates to a particular object under consideration. For instance, your name, weight, height, weights are unique to you. You can also consider a file, image, or picture as data.

Definition Database

A database is a systematical collection of data. Through a database, you can manipulate and manage data easily. For instance, your electricity supply has a database to manage your billing, address, and other relevant information. Another example is your famous Facebook account; it contains information relating to your friends, messages, member activities, pictures, etc.

Definition Database Management System

DBMS is a collection of programs enables users to access database, report, manipulate, and represent data. Furthermore, it allows users to control access to the database. DBMS is not a new concept and was first implemented in the 1960s.

Types of Database Management System

- *Hierarchical DBMS* – this uses a "parent-child" relationship in storing data. People hardly use them nowadays. However, it has the structure of a tree with nodes representing records. An example of this type of DBMS is the registry used in Windows XP

- *Network DBMS* – This DBMS allows many-to-many relationship. For beginners, this is a complicated database structure. An example is the RDM server.

- *Relational DBMS* – This kind of DBMS defines a database relationship in terms of tables. Unlike the network DBMS, relational DBMS doesn't allow many-to-many relationship. Example of relational DBMS includes a Microsoft SQL Server database, Oracle, and MySQL.

- Object-Oriented Relation DBMS – *This allows the storage of new data types. Data are stored in the form of objects*

Setting Your SQL Work Environment

Peradventure you don't have any database management system in your computer, you can opt for various free open source database management system. You can decide to opt for the famous MySQL, which can be downloaded for both Windows and Linux operating systems.

Furthermore, you can install SQL Server Express, which is a free version of Microsoft SQL Server. Otherwise, you can decide to install XAMPP or WampServer. The

WampServer is a Windows web development environment that allows you to create a MySQL database, PHP, and Apache2.

SQL Syntax

SQL Statements – These statements are simple and straightforward like your normal English language. However, they have specific syntax. Don't form your own meaning when you see some of the common English words you are conversant within this chapter.

An SQL statement comprises of a series of keywords, identifiers, etc. and ends with a semicolon (;). The following is an example of a SQL statement:

```
SELECT stu_name, DoB, age FROM studentFile Where age > 20;
```

The statement may look clumsy but for better readability, you can rewrite it in this format.

```
SELECT stu_name, DoB, age

FROM StudentFile

WHERE age > 20;
```

The purpose of the semicolon is to submit the statement to the database server or terminates the SQL statement.

Case Sensitivity in SQL

Keywords in SQL are not case sensitive like the previous languages discussed in this book. For instance, the keyword SELECT is the same as the select. However, depending on the operating system, the table names and database can be case-sensitive. Generally, Linux and UNIX platforms are case-sensitive, unlike Windows platforms that are not case-sensitive.

The example below retrieves records from the studentFile table

SELECT stu_name, DoB, age FROM studentFile;
select stu_name, DoB, age from studentFile;

The first one capitalizes the keywords whereas the second isn't capitalized. It is better to write SQL keywords in uppercase in order to differentiate it from other text.

SQL Comments

Similar to other programming languages, SQL comments are ignored and provide quick explanations concerning the SQL statements. You can either use a single-line or multi-line comments when writing comments in SQL. The two examples below will distinguish both comment writing formats.

```
--Select all the students

SELECT *FROM studentFile;
```

To write a multi-line comment, you use the /* with the statements followed by the */.

```
/* Select all the students

 whose age is greater than 20*/

SELECT *FROM studentFile

WHERE age > 20;
```

Database Creation

Before you can work with data, the first thing to do is to create a database. I am assuming you have installed the

SQL Server or have MySQL in your system. Furthermore, ensure to allow every necessary privilege needed.

There are two ways of creating a database

- Using the simple SQL query
- *Using MySQL*

Simple SQL Query

The syntax for creating a database in SQL is

```
CREATE DATABASE databaseName;
```

```
CREATE DATABASE studentFile;
```

Note: You can also use CREATE SCHEMA rather than using CREATE DATABASE to create a database. Additionally, creating a database doesn't make it available for use. To select the database, you have to select the database using the USE statement. For instance, the USE studentFile; command will set the StudentFile database as the target database.

MySQL Database Creation

I will use a command line tool to create a database in MySQL.

Step 1: Invoking the MySQL command-line tool

To do this, you have to log into your MySQL server. You have to log in as a root user and enter your password when asked. If everything goes right, you will be able to issue SQL statements.

Step 2: Creating the database

To create the database "studentFile", you have to execute the following command.

```
mysql> CREATE DATABASE studentFile;
```

If the database was successful, you will see – Query OK, 1 row affected (0.03 sec). However, if the database already exists, an error message will display. Therefore, to avoid such situation, you can include an optional clause – IF NOT EXISTS. To apply it to the example, it will be written as:

```
mysql> CREATE DATABASE IF NOT EXISTS studentFile;
```

Step 3: Selecting the Database

If the database already exists and you use the IF NOT EXISTS statement, to select this new database as the default database, you have to select it.

```
mysql > USE studentFile;
```

Tip – in order to see all the list of existing databases when using MySQL server, you can use the "SHOW DATABASES" keyword to execute it.

Creating Tables in SQL

So far, I am convinced you now know how to create a database. It is time to upgrade your knowledge in SQL by creating a table inside our database. The table will hold the data in the database. The purpose of the table is to organize your data or information into columns and rows.

The syntax for table creation

CREATE TABLE tableName (

Column1_name data_type constraints,

Column2_name data_type constraints,

Column3_name data_type constraints,

    );

For better understanding, I will create a table in our studentFile database using the MySQL command-line tool. The code below simplifies that.

```
-- Syntax for MySQL Database

CREATE TABLE studentRecord (

    id INT NOT NULL PRIMARY KEY AUTO_INCREMENT,

    Studname VARCHAR(50) NOT NULL,

    DoB DATE,

    phoneNum VARCHAR(15) NOT NULL UNIQUE

-- Syntax for SQL Server Database

CREATE TABLE studentRecord (

    id INT NOT NULL PRIMARY KEY IDENTITY(1,1),

    Studname VARCHAR(50) NOT NULL,

    DoB DATE,

    phoneNum VARCHAR(15) NOT NULL UNIQUE

);
```

The code above creates a table named studentRecord with five columns id, Studname, DoB, and phoneNum. If you observe, a data type declaration succeeds each column name.

In a database table, every column must have a name followed by a data type. The developer decides on the particular to use, depending on the information to store in each column. From the example above, some statement looks "foreign" and requires explanations. Later, I will talk about the various data types but to familiarize yourself with them, they include:

- Exact numeric
- Approximate numeric
- Date and time
- Character strings
- Unicode character strings
- Binary strings
- Other data types

Besides the data type, there are constraints used in the code. Constraints are rules defined concerning the values permitted in columns. The following constraints were mentioned.

- The PRIMARY KEY constrains, which marks the corresponding field as the primary key for the table
- The NOT NULL constraints, which make sure fields cannot accept an unacceptable value
- The AUTO_INCREMENT attribute, which automatically assigns a value to a field left unspecified. It increases the previous value by 1 and only available for numerical fields.
- *The UNIQUE constraint ensures every single row contains a unique value in the table*

In a similar fashion, you can use the IF NOT EXIST statement we used when creating a database to overwrite an existing table. This is important as it avoids any already existing table. Alternatively, if you want to display available tables, you can use the SHOW TABLES statement.

```
CREATE TABLE IF NOT EXISTS studentRecords (

    id INT NOT NULL PRIMARY KEY AUTO_INCREMENT,

    Studname VARCHAR(40) NOT NULL, DoB,

    phoneNum VARCHAR(25) NOT NULL UNIQUE

);
```

Constraints In SQL

As the name implies, it is a restriction or limitation imposed on a column (s) of a table in order to place a limitation on the type of values the table can store. They provide a better mechanism to retain the reliability and accuracy of the data contained in the table. We have several categories of constraints, which includes:

NOT NULL Constraint – This statement states that NULL values will not be accepted at the column. What it means is that a new row cannot be added in a table without the inclusion of a non-NULL value for such a column.

For instance, the statement below creates a table "studentRecords" with four columns and three of these columns (id, Studname, and phoneNum) do not accept NULL Values.

```
CREATE TABLE studentRecords (
    id INT NOT NULL,
    Studname VARCHAR(30) NOT NULL,
    DoB DATE,
    phoneNum VARCHAR(15) NOT NULL
);
```

Tip: A null value is not the same as blank, zero (0), or a zero-length character string. The meaning of a NULL is that there hasn't been any entry made in that field.

- PRIMARY KEY Constraint – *This classifies a column (s) with values that distinctively recognize a row in the table. You cannot have two rows simultaneously in a particular table having the same value for its primary key. The example below shows a SQL statement creating a table named "studentRecords" and identify the id column as the primary key.*

```
CREATE TABLE studentRecords (

   id INT NOT NULL PRIMARY KEY,

   Studname VARCHAR(30) NOT NULL,

   DoB DATE,

   phoneNum VARCHAR(15) NOT NULL
);
```

- UNIQUE Constraint – *if you want to restrict a column (s) to contain unique values in a table, the UNIQUE statement is used. While the PRIMARY KEY and UNIQUE constraint enforce uniqueness in a table; however, the UNIQUE constraint is used when your goal is to enforce the exclusivity on a particular column (s). I will use our previous example to specify the phone column as unique. With this, the phone column won't allow duplicated values.*

```
CREATE TABLE studentRecords (

  id INT NOT NULL PRIMARY KEY,

  Studname VARCHAR(30) NOT NULL,

  DoB DATE,

  phoneNum VARCHAR(15) NOT NULL UNIQUE,

    country  VARCHAR(30)  NOT  NULL  DEFAULT
'England'

);
```

- *FOREIGN KEY Constraint* – This particular kind of constraint is a column (s) used to set up and implement a relationship among data in two different tables.
- CHECK constraint – *The purpose of this statement is to restrict values in a column. For instance, the range of student age column can be restricted by creating CHECK constraint, which allows values only 16 to 45. This hinders*

ages entered from exceeding the age range. Here is an example to illustrate it.

```
CREATE TABLE studentRecords (

   stu_id INT NOT NULL PRIMARY KEY,

   stu_name VARCHAR(55) NOT NULL,

   stu_date DATE NOT NULL,

   age INT NOT NULL CHECK (age >= 16 AND age <= 45),

   dept_id INT,

       FOREIGN    KEY    (dept_id)    REFERENCES departments(dept_id)

);
```

Inserting Data in Tables

In previous examples, I created a table with the name "studentRecords" in our "studentFile" database. Now, we need to add information into the table. To do this, SQL has a unique keyword, which is the "INSERT INTO" statement.

Format:

INSERT INTO NameOfTable (columnA, columnB, columnC,...) VALUES (value1, value2, value3,...);

The syntax is self-explanatory but if you are unclear, the tableName is the name of your table. In our examples so far, we have used "studentRecords." However, the column1, column2, column3,... represents the name of the table columns with value1, value2, value3 the parallel values for the columns.

To insert records to our "studentRecords" table, we will use the following statement.

```
INSERT INTO studentRecords (FullName, Age, Sex, PhoneNum) ;

VALUES ('Donald Williamson', '30', 'Male', '0722-022569') ;
```

If you observe, there is no value inserted for the id field. Do you remember when we created the table (studentRecords), we mark the id field with an AUTO_INCREMENT flag. Let's add another record to our table.

```
INSERT INTO studentRecords (FullName, Age, Sex,
PhoneNum) ;

VALUES ('Jefferson Peterson', '45', 'Male', '0252-
027948') ;
```

Why don't you add another one?

```
INSERT INTO studentRecords (FullName, Age, Sex,
PhoneNum) ;

VALUES ('Mariah Lawson', '50', 'Female', '0722-
457906') ;
```

If you were to display the output of this table, it will look like this

id	FullName	Age	Sex	PhoneNum
1	Donald Williamson	30	Male	0722-022569
2	Jefferson Peterson	45	Male	0252-027948
3	Mariah Lawson	50	Female	0722-457906

Chapter 1: Creating a Database in SQL Server

Like I mentioned above, SQL databases are among the most used databases across the world. This is because of a number of reasons, for instance it is very easy to create. What you need is a graphical user interface program that comes freely like a SQL Server Management. With that in place, creating a database is easy and you can start entering your data in no time at all. Here is how:

1. **Start by installing the software(SQL Server Management Studio) to your computer**

This is software that is freely available for Microsoft. It will allow you to gain access to and also to work with your SQL server from a graphical interface other than using a command line for the same. The software will also allow you to gain access to a remote request of an SQL server. If not this one, you will require a similar software.

There are other interfaces that are available for other platforms like Mac for instance SQuirreL SQL. Such interfaces may differ but they all work the same.

You can also create a database using the tools available in command line.

2. **Once the software has been installed, start it up.**

After the installation, you can now start your program. You will be required to choose if you want to connect to a certain server. If there is a server already that is already set and working and you have all the permissions connect access it, just enter its address and the authentication information. But if you want to build your own local database, you will create the Database name and the type of authentication under the **Windows Authentication**.

3. **Now locate your database folder**

After a connection has been made to the server, whether it is a local connection or a remote one, the Object Explorer will now open on the left hand side of your screen. Right at the top part of your Object Explorer diagram, you will see the server that you are using to.

If it has not been expanded, click on the "+" icon that is following it and it will expand.

4. **You can now create a fresh database**

Spot the database folder and right click on it. Click on New database option from the list that will come up. This will give you a new window which will allow you to organize your database before you start creating it. First of all, you need to give your database a new and unique name, which will make it easy for you to identify it. The other settings can be left just the way they are at default settings unless there is an important change that you want to make. When you give your database a name, there are two other additional files that will be formed automatically, which are log and data files. The data file will be the one that will host all your information in your database and the log file will be the one that will track all the changes that you will make on the database. When satisfied, you can hit OK in order to create your database. Your newly created database will now appear in the extended database Folder, with a cylindrical icon, it will be easy to spot it.

5. **Start creating your table**

You have to come up with a structure where you will start storing your data and this will be your table. With a table, you can hold all manner of information and data that you want stored in the database. This is an important part before you can go on. To do this, you enlarge the new database that is in your database folder and then right click on the table's icon to select a New Table option. Windows thereafter opens everything else on your screen to let you to work on your new table as much as you want.

6. It's time for the primary key

Primary keys are very important, therefore it is important to let them be the first entry on the first column of your SQL table. They act as the ID number or the highest number that helps you quickly remember what you have put in record in that table. In order to create your primary keys, enter ID on the field that has the Column Name and enter INT into the field marked Data Type. As of the Allow Nulls, ensure that they are all unchecked. Now hit the key icon in your toolbar in order to make this column your primary key. With this, you will not have null values but if you want to have a null value as your principal entry, you will check to Allow Nulls.

Scroll down the column properties to find the option Identity Specification. Expanding this option and setting it to a YES will ensure that the values on the ID column increases automatically on every entry that you will make. With this, all your new entries will be effectively numbered in the right order.

7. **It's time to understand how tables are designed**

This is an important part so as to find it easy to enter information in your database. With tables, you will get different columns or fields and every column denotes an aspect of every database entry that you will make. If you have a database for people in an organization for instance, your will have a FirsName column entry, LastName column entry, Address, Phone Number and such like entries.

8. **The other columns**

When all the fields of the Primary Key have been filled in, other fields will automatically form beneath it. These will be the fields where all your other data will be entered. You are now free to enter data in those fields the way you want to. The right data type has to be chosen though so that it will match the data that you have filled in that column.

nchar(#) represents the type of data that should be used for the text for instance addresses, names among others. In the parenthesis will be a number which is the highest number that will be allowed in that field. You can set the limit in order to allow the size of your database to remain manageable. You can for instance use this format for the phone numbers in order to make it hard for you to perform mathematical function on the numbers.

int on the other hand represents data in whole numbers. This is the one that is used in the field marked ID.

decimal(x,y) will save your numbers in a decimal format. The number within the parenthesis will signify the total number of numerals and the other number of digits that will follow the decimals respectively.

9. **When all that is done, save the table**

First save the table then you can start entering information on your columns. To do this, click on the Save button on your toolbar, then enter the name for your table. It is important to have a unique and easy to understand name for your table so that you will be able to tell what the table is all about without going through the data in it. This will be very useful especially once you start using large databases that have so many tables.

Chapter 2: The SQL Structure

In this chapter you will learn the fundamental features of the SQL language and an overview of its programming aspect. In addition, you will be presented with a step-by-step instruction on where and how to download SQLite, a version of the SQL software that will be used all throughout the discussion of this e-Book.

SQL Fundamental Features

SQL is a flexible computer language that you can deploy in different ways to communicate with relational databases. This software has some distinct features that differentiates it from other programming applications. First and foremost, SQL is a nonprocedural language. Most computer programs (e.g., C, C++ and Java) solve problems by following a sequence of commands that is called a *procedure*. In this case, one specific operation is performed after another until the required task has been accomplished. The flow of operation can either be a linear sequence or a looping one, depending on what the programmer had specified. This is not the same for SQL. In using this application, you will just have to specify the output that you want, not how you want to generate the output. From the CUSTOMER TABLE, if you want to create a separate list of contacts whose company are located in Texas then you have to retrieve the rows where the STATE column contains "TX" as its value. In writing the SQL command, you don't have to indicate how the information should be retrieved. It is the primary role of the database management system to examine the database and decide how to generate the results you wanted.

Learning the SQL syntax is like understanding the English language structure. Its command language, comprised of a limited number of statements, performs three primary data functions - definition, manipulation and control. The SQL programming language also includes reserved words that are only to be used for specific purposes. Thus, you cannot use these words as names for variables, tables and columns; or in any other way apart from their intended use. Below are some of the most common reserved words in SQL:2011.

ABS	ALL	ALLOCATE	ALTER	AND	ANY
ARE	ARRAY	AS	AT	AVG	BEGIN
BETWEEN	BINARY	BOOLEAN	BOTH	BY	CALL
CASCADED	CASE	CEILING	CHAR	CHARACTER	CHECK
CLOSE	COLLATE	COLLECT	COLUMN	COMMIT	CONDITION
CONNECT	CONSTRAINT	CONVERT	COUNT	CREATE	CURSOR
CYCLE	DATE	DAY	DEALLOCATE	DEC	DECIMAL
DECLARE	DEFAULT	DELETE	DESCRIBE	DISCONNECT	DISTINCT
DOUBLE	DROP	DYNAMIC	EACH	ELEMENT	ELSE
END	ESCAPE	EVERY	EXCEPT	EXECUTE	EXISTS
EXTERNAL	EXTRACT	FALSE	FETCH	FILTER	FLOAT
FLOOR	FOR	FOREVER	FREE	FROM	FULL
FUNCTION	FUSION	GET	GLOBAL	GRANT	GROUP
GROUPING	HAVING	HOLD	HOUR	HOURS	IDENTITY
IN	INNER	INOUT	INSERT	INT	INTEGER
INTERSECT	INTERVAL	INTO	IS	JOIN	KEEP
LANGUAGE	LARGE	LEAD	LEFT	LIKE	LOCAL

LOWER	MATCH	MAX	MEMBER	MERGE	METHOD
MINUTE	MOD	MODULE	MONTH	MULTISET	NATIONAL
NATURAL	NEW	NIL	NO	NONE	NORMALIZE
NOT	NULL	NUMERIC	OF	OFFSET	OLD
ON	ONLY	OPEN	OR	ORDER	OUT
OVER	OVERLAY	PARAMETER	PARTITION	POSITION	POWER
PRECISION	PREPARE	PRIMARY	PROCEDURE	RANGE	RANK
REAL	RECURSIVE	REF	REFERENCES	REFERENCING	RELEASE
RESULT	RETURN	REVOKE	RIGHT	ROLLBACK	ROLLUP
ROW	ROWS	SCOPE	SCROLL	SEARCH	SECOND
SELECT	SET	SIMILAR	SOME	SPECIFIC	SQL
START	STATIC	SUM	SYMMETRIC	SYSTEM	TABLE
THEN	TIME	TIMESTAMP	TO	TRANSLATE	TREAT
TRIGGER	TRUNCATE	TRIM	TRUE	UNION	UNIQUE
UNKNOWN	UPDATE	UPPER	USER	USING	VALUE
VALUES	VARCHAR	VARYING	VERSION	WHEN	WHENEVER
WHERE	WINDOW	WITH	WITHIN	WITHOUT	YEAR

If you think that an SQL database is just a collection of tables, then you are wrong. There are additional structures that need to be specified to maintain the integrity of your data, such as schemas, domains and constraints.

- *Schema* – This is also called the *conceptual view* or the *complete logical view* that defines the entire database structure and provides overall table organization. Such schema is considered a metadata – stored in tables and part of the database (just like tables that consist of regular data).

- *Domain* – This specifies the set of all finite data values you can store in a particular table column or attribute. For example, in our previous CUSTOMER TABLE the STATE column can only contain the values "TX", "NY", "CA" and "NV" if you only provide products and services in the states of Texas, New York, California and Nevada respectively. So these four state abbreviations are the domain of the STATE attribute.

- *Constraint* – Often ignored but one of the important database components, this sets down the rules that identify what data values a specific table attribute can contain. Incorporating tight constraints assures that database users only enter valid data into a particular column. Together with defined table characteristics, column constraints determine its domain. Using the same STATE column as an example with the given constraint of only the four values, if a database user enters "NJ" for New Jersey, then the entry will not be accepted. The system will not proceed until a valid value is entered for the STATE attribute, unless the database structure needs to be updated due to sudden business changes.

ROLLBACK [WORK];

In the previous command line, the keyword *WORK* is optional.

- *SAVEPOINT* – This statement works with the ROLLBACK command, wherein it creates sections or points within groups of transactions in which you will be performing the ROLLBACK command. Its syntax is:

SAVEPOINT *SAVEPOINT_NAME*;

> SQLite Installation Instructions and Database
> Features

Before you start overwhelming yourself with various database solutions and SQL command lines, you need to determine first your purpose why you are creating a database. This will further determine other database design considerations such as size, complexity, type of machine where the application will run, storage medium and more. When you start thinking of your database requirements, you need to know up to what level of detail should be considered in your design. Too much detail will result to a very complex design that further wastes time and effort, and even your computer's storage space. Too little will lead to a poor performing, corrupt and worthless database. Once you are done with the design phase, then you can decide which database software you can download to start your SQL experience.

For the sake of this e-Book's discussion, SQLite, a simple software library, will be used as a starter database engine to design, build and deploy applications. A free and stand-alone database software that is quick to download and easy to administer, SQLite was developed by Richard Hipp and his team of programmers. It is was designed so that it can be easily configured and implemented, which does not require any client-server setup at all. Thus, SQLite is considered as one of the most widely used database software applications in the world.

Stated below are some of the major features of SQLite:

- Transactions are atomic, consistent, isolated and durable
- Compilation is simple and easy
- System crashes and power failures are supported
- Full SQL implementation with a stand-alone command-line interface client
- Code footprint is significantly small
- Adaptable and adjustable to larger projects
- Self-contained with no external dependencies
- ***Portable and supports other platforms like Windows, Android, iOS, Mac, Solaris and more***

In using SQLite, you need to download *SQLiteStudio* as your database manager and editor. With its intuitive interface, this software is very light yet fast and powerful. You don't even need to install it, just download, unpack and run the application. Follow these simple steps in downloading SQLiteStudio on a Windows 10 computer:

1. **Go to** http://sqlitestudio.pl/?act=about. **You should get the following page:**

2. Check the version of your computer's operating system then click the appropriate link to start downloading the software.

After downloading the software, go to the folder where the application was saved (usually the Downloads Folder in Windows). Click on the *Extract* tab on top then choose the *Extract all* option.

You will get the *Extract Compressed (Zipped) Folders* dialog box. Change the destination folder to C:\SQL then click the *Extract* button. This will be the folder where all your SQLite files will be saved.

5. Once all the files have been extracted, you will have the SQLiteStudio subfolder.

6. Find the application program named SQLiteStudio inside the subfolder. To create a shortcut on your desktop (so you can quickly launch the application), right-click the

filename, select *Send to* option then choose *Desktop (create shortcut)*.

7. When you double-click the SQLiteStudio icon on your desktop,

8. **you should get the following screen:**

Chapter 3: Database Administration

Once you have your database up and running with tables and queries it is up you to keep the production database running smoothly. The database will have to be regularly looked at in order to ensure that it continues to perform as originally intended. If a database is poorly maintained it can easily result in a website connected to it performing poorly or worse still result in down time or even data loss. There is usually a person designated to look after the database and their job is titled Database Administrator or DBA. However, it's usually a non-DBA person who needs help with the database.

There are a number of different tasks which you can perform when carrying out maintenance which include the following:

Database Integrity: When you check the integrity of the database you are running checks on the data to make sure that both the physical and logical structure of the database is consistent and accurate.

Index Reorganization: Once you start to insert and delete data on your database there is going to be fragmentation (or a scattering) of indexes. Reorganizing the index will bring everything back together again and increase speed.

Rebuild Index: You don't have to perform an index reorganization, you can drop an index and then recreate them.

Database Backup: One of the most important tasks to perform. There are a number of different ways in which you can back up the database, these include: Full which backs up the database entirely, Differential which backs up the database since the last full backup and Transaction log which only backs up the transactional log.

Check Database Statistics: You can check the statistics of the database which are kept on queries. If you update the statistics, which can get out of date, you can help aid the queries being run.

Data and Log File: In general, make sure the data and log files are kept separate from each other. These files will grow when your database is being used and its best to allocate them an appropriate size going forward (and not just enable them to grow).

Depending on your database some tasks may be more useful than others. Apart from database backup which probably mandatory if it's in production you can pick through the other tasks depending on the state of the database.

For example, should the fragmentation of the database be below 30% then you can choose to perform an index reorganization. However, if the database fragmentation is greater than 30% then you should rebuild the index. You can rebuild the index on a weekly basis or more often if possible.

You can run a maintenance plan on SQL Server via its Server Agent depending on database requirements. It's important to set the times right not when your application is expected to be busy. You can choose a time or you can run it when the server CPU is not busy. Choosing to run when the server is not busy is a more preferred option for larger databases than selecting a particular time as there is no guaranteed time which the CPU will be idle. However, it is usually only a concern if your application is quite big and has a lot of requests.

When you do rebuild the indexes, it is important that you have the results sorted in tempdb. When using tempdb the old indexes are kept until new ones are added. Normally rebuilding the indexes uses the fixed space which the database was allocated. So, if you run out of disk space then you would not be able to complete the rebuilding of indexes. It's possible to use the tempdb and not have to increase the database disk size. The database maintenance can be run both synchronous (wait for task completion) or asynchronous (together) to speed things up however you must make sure that the tasks run in the right order.

Setting up a maintenance plan in SQL Server

To set up a maintenance plan in SQL Server you first must get the server to show advanced options. This is done by running the following code in a new query in SQL Server:

sp_configure 'show advanced options', 1

GO

RECONFIGURE

GO

sp_configure 'Agent XPs', 1

GO

RECONFIGURE

GO

SQL Server will now display the advanced options. Left click the + icon to the left of Management which is on the left-hand side of SQL Server Management Studio. Now left click Maintenance Plans and then right click Maintenance Plans. Select New Maintenance Plan Wizard.

Enter an appropriate maintenance plan name and description. From here you can either run one or all tasks in one plan and have as many plans as you want. After you have given a name, choose single schedule and click next.

You will see a number of options which you can pick for your maintenance including: *Check Database Integrity, Shrink Database, Reorganize Index, Rebuild Index, Update Statistics, Clean up History, Execute SQL Server Agent Job, Back Up – full, differential or transaction log and Maintenance Cleanup Task*. Select which you want to perform (in this example select all) This wizard will bring you through each of the items you have selected to fine tune them.

Once you select the items you want in your plan click next, you can now rearrange them in the order you wish them to complete. It's best to have Database Backup first in case of power failure, so select it and move it to the top of the list. Click next.

Define Back Up Database (Full) Task

This screen allows you to pick which full database backup you wish to perform it on. Best practice is to keep one plan per database, select one database and select next.

Define Database Check Integrity Task

This screen – the integrity task is a SQL Server command which checks the integrity of the database to see if everything is not corrupt and stable. Select a database and click next.

Define Shrink Database Task

You can now configure to shrink the database in order to free up space in the next screen. It will only shrink space if available but should you need space in the future you will have to re allocate it. However, this step will help backup speeds. Most developers don't use this feature that much. Click next after selecting a database to shrink.

Define Reorganize Index Task

The next screen is the Define Reorganize Index Tag screen. When you add, modify and delete indexes you will, like tables, need to reorganize them. The process is the same as a hard disk where you have there are fragmented files and space scattered across the disk. Best practice is to perform this task once per week for a busy database. You can choose to compact large object which compacts any index which has large binary object data. Click next to proceed to the next screen.

Define Rebuild Index Task

This screen covers individual index rows. As mentioned either reorganize or reindexing. Doing both together in one plan is pointless. Depending on your fragmentation level pick one or the other. In this example select your database and sort results in tempdb. Click next to proceed.

Define Update Statistics Task

The update statistics task helps developer keep track of data retrieval as its created, modified and deleted. You can keep the statistics up to date by performing this plan. Both statistics for index and statistics for individual columns are kept. Select your database and click next to proceed.

Define History Cleanup Task

You should now see the Define maintenance cleanup task screen which specifies the historical data to delete. You can specify a shorter time frame to keep the backup and recovery, agent job history and maintenance place for on the drop down. Click next to proceed.

Define Back up Database (Differential) Task

This screen allows you to back up every page in the database which has been changed since the last full backup. Select a database you wish to use and click next.

Define Back Up Database (Transaction Log) Task

The transaction log backup backs up all the log records since the last backup. You can choose a folder to store it. Performing this type of backup is the least resource intensive backup. Select a database and storage location and click next.

Define Execute SQL Server Agent Job Task

The SQL Server Agent Job Task deals with jobs that are outside the wizard, for example it could be to check for nulls, check whether the database meets specified standards etc. Any jobs that are specified in SQL Server Agent Job Task are listed here. Click next to proceed.

Define Maintenance Cleanup Task

This screen defines the clean-up action of the maintenance task i.e. to ensure that the they are not taking up unnecessary space, so you can specify where to store them. You can delete specific backup files. Click next to proceed.

Report Options

The next screen covers where you want to store the report of the maintenance plan. Make a note of where you are going to store it. You need to have email set up on SQL Server in order to email it. Click next to proceed.

Complete the Wizard

The final screen is a complete review of the wizard. You can review the summary of the plan and which options were selected. Clicking finishes ends the wizard and creates the plan. You should now see a success screen with the tasks completed.

Running the maintenance plan

Once you successfully complete the maintenance wizard the next step is to run the plan you created. In order to get the plan to run you need to have the SQL Server Agent running. It is visible two down from where Management is on SQL Server Management Studio. You can left click SQL Server Agent and then right click and select Start.

Also, you can press the windows key + and press the letter r, then type in services.msc and hit return. Once Services appear scroll down and look for SQL Server Agent (MSSQLEXPRESS). SQL Server Express was installed in this EBook but you can select the other versions like (MSSQLSERVER) if you installed that. Left click it, then right click it and select Start.

You can go back to SSMS and right click on the maintenance plan you created under maintenance plans and then select Execute. This will now run your plan. One successful completion of the plan click ok and close the dialogue box. You can view the reports by right clicking the maintenance plan you created and selecting View history. On the left-hand side are all the different plans in SQL Server while on the right is the results of the specific plan.

Emailing the reports.

A lot of DBA's like to get their database reports via email. What you need to do is to set up a database mail before you can fire off emails and then set up a Server agent to send the email.

Setting up Database Mail.

The first step is to right click Database mail in SSMS and select configure database mail. A wizard screen will appear, click next. Now select the first choice – set up Database Mail and click next. Enter a profile name optional description of the profile. Now click on the Add button to the right.

This will bring you to an add New Database Mail Account – SMTP. You need to enter the STMP details for an email account. Maybe you can set up a new email account for this service. You can search online for SMTP details, Gmail works quite well (server name: smtp.gmail.com, port number 587, SSL required, tick basic authentication & confirm password). Click on ok. Click next, click on public (important: so it can be used by the rest of the database). Set it as default profile, click next, click next again. You should now get a success screen. Click close.

SQL Server Agent

To send off the database email you need to set up a Server Agent. Start by right clicking on SQL Server Agent – New – Operator. Give the operator a name like Maintenance Plan Operator and enter in the email address you wish to send the report to and click ok.

Now right the maintenance plan that you have successfully executed and select modify. The maintenance plan design screen will appear on the right-hand side where you can see some graphics of the tasks completed in it. Now click on Reporting and Logging – it is an icon situated on the menu bar of the design plan - to the left of Manage Connections...

The Reporting and Logging window will appear. Select the tick box – Send report to an email recipient and select the Maintenance plan operator you just created. The next time you run the plan an email will be sent to the email address.

Summary

The running and maintenance of a database is an important job. Having the right plan for your database means it will continue to work as originally designed and you can quickly identify database errors or slowdowns early on and fix them quickly.

Chapter 4: Structure of the SELECT Statement

The SELECT Clause

The SELECT clause is the only required clause in a SELECT statement, all the other clauses are optional. The SELECT columns can be literals (constants), expressions, table columns and even subqueries. Lines can be commented with "--".

```
SELECT                    15           *
15;                              -- 225

SELECT Today = convert(DATE, getdate());   -
- 2016-07-27

SELECT                Color,

                ProdCnt             =
COUNT(*),

                AvgPrice            =
FORMAT(AVG(ListPrice),'c','en-US')

FROM AdventureWorks2012.Production.Product p

WHERE Color is not null
```

```
GROUP BY Color   HAVING count(*) > 10

ORDER BY AvgPrice DESC;

GO
```

Color	ProdCnt	AvgPrice
Yellow	36	$959.09
Blue	26	$923.68
Silver	43	$850.31
Black	93	$725.12
Red	38	$1,401.95

```
-- Equivalent with column aliases on the right

SELECT                          Color,

                    COUNT(*)
           AS ProdCnt,

                    FORMAT(AVG(ListPrice),'c','en-
US')           AS AvgPrice

FROM AdventureWorks2012.Production.Product p

WHERE Color is not null  GROUP BY Color
```

HAVING count(*) > 10

ORDER BY AvgPrice DESC;

GO

SELECT with Search Expression

SELECT statement can have complex expressions for text or numbers as demonstrated in the next T-SQL query for finding the street name in AddressLine1 column.

```
SELECT          AddressID,

          SUBSTRING(AddressLine1, CHARINDEX('
', AddressLine1+' ', 1) +1,

               CHARINDEX(' ',  AddressLine1+' ',
CHARINDEX(' ', AddressLine1+' ', 1) +1) -

          CHARINDEX(' ', AddressLine1+' ', 1) -
1)                                        AS
StreetName,

          AddressLine1,

     City

FROM AdventureWorks2012.Person.Address
```

WHERE ISNUMERIC (LEFT(AddressLine1,1))=1

 AND City = 'Seattle'

ORDER BY AddressLine1;

-- -- (141 row(s) affected)- Partial results.

AddressID	StreetName	AddressLine1	City
13079	boulevard	081, boulevard du Montparnasse	Seattle
859	Oak	1050 Oak Street	Seattle
110	Slow	1064 Slow Creek Road	Seattle
113	Ravenwood	1102 Ravenwood	Seattle
95	Bradford	1220 Bradford Way	Seattle
32510	Steven	1349 Steven Way	Seattle
118	Balboa	136 Balboa Court	Seattle
32519	Mazatlan	137 Mazatlan	Seattle
25869	Calle	1386 Calle Verde	Seattle
114	Yorba	1398 Yorba Linda	Seattle
15657	Book	151 Book Ct	Seattle
105	Stillman	1619 Stillman Court	Seattle
18002	Carmel	1635 Carmel Dr	Seattle

19813	Acardia	1787 Acardia Pl.	Seattle
16392	Orchid	1874 Orchid Ct	Seattle
18053	Green	1883 Green View Court	Seattle
13035	Mt.	1887 Mt. Diablo St	Seattle
29864	Valley	1946 Valley Crest Drive	Seattle
13580	Hill	2030 Hill Drive	Seattle
106	San	2144 San Rafael	Seattle

SELECT Statement with Subquery

Two Northwind category images, Beverages & Dairy Products, from the dbo.Categories table.

The following SELECT statement involves a subquery which is called a derived table. It also demonstrates that INNER JOIN can be performed with a GROUP BY subquery as well not only with another table or view.

```
USE Northwind;

SELECT          c.CategoryName
                    AS Category,

            cnum.NoOfProducts
        AS CatProdCnt,

                p.ProductName
                AS Product,

                FORMAT(p.UnitPrice,'c', 'en-
US')                AS UnitPrice

FROM    Categories c

                INNER JOIN Products p

                    ON c.CategoryID =
p.CategoryID

                        INNER      JOIN
(       SELECT          c.CategoryID,

    NoOfProducts = count(* )

                        FROM    Ca
tegories c
```

```
                                                    INNER
JOIN Products p

                                                       ON
c.CategoryID = p.CategoryID

                                              GROUP BY
c.CategoryID

                                                        )
cnum                                          -- derived
table

                                    ON c.CategoryID =
cnum.CategoryID

ORDER BY Category, Product;

-- (77 row(s) affected) - Partial results.
```

Category	CatProdCnt	Product	UnitPrice
Dairy Products	10	Mozzarella di Giovanni	$34.80
Dairy Products	10	Queso Cabrales	$21.00

Dairy Products	10	Queso Manchego La Pastora	$38.00
Dairy Products	10	Raclette Courdavault	$55.00
Grains/Cereals	7	Filo Mix	$7.00
Grains/Cereals	7	Gnocchi di nonna Alice	$38.00
Grains/Cereals	7	Gustaf's Knäckebröd	$21.00
Grains/Cereals	7	Ravioli Angelo	$19.50
Grains/Cereals	7	Singaporean Hokkien Fried Mee	$14.00
Grains/Cereals	7	Tunnbröd	$9.00

Creating Delimited String List (CSV) with XML PATH

The XML PATH clause , the text() function and correlated subquery is used to create a comma delimited string within the SELECT columns. Note: it cannot be done using traditional (without XML) SQL single statement, it can be done with multiple SQL statements only. STUFF() string function is applied to replace the leading comma with an empty string

```
USE AdventureWorks;

SELECT          Territory          = st.[Name],

                SalesYTD =   FORMAT(floor(SalesYTD),
'c', 'en-US'), -- currency format

                SalesStaffAssignmentHistory =

                STUFF((SELECT CONCAT(', ', c.FirstName,
SPACE(1), c.LastName)     AS [text()]

                                FROM   Person.Contact c

                                INNER          JOIN
Sales.SalesTerritoryHistory sth
```

```
                        ON    c.ContactID    =
sth.SalesPersonID

                           WHERE   sth.TerritoryID
=   st.TerritoryID

                    ORDER  BY StartDate

                    FOR  XML Path (")), 1, 1,
SPACE(0))

FROM   Sales.SalesTerritory st

ORDER  BY SalesYTD DESC;

GO
```

Territory	SalesYTD	SalesStaffAssignmentHistory
Southwest	$8,351,296.00	Shelley Dyck, Jauna Elson
Canada	$6,917,270.00	Carla Eldridge, Michael Emanuel, Gail Erickson
Northwest	$5,767,341.00	Shannon Elliott, Terry Eminhizer, Martha Espinoza

Central	$4,677,108.00	Linda Ecoffey, Maciej Dusza
France	$3,899,045.00	Mark Erickson
Northeast	$3,857,163.00	Maciej Dusza, Linda Ecoffey
United Kingdom	$3,514,865.00	Michael Emanuel
Southeast	$2,851,419.00	Carol Elliott
Germany	$2,481,039.00	Janeth Esteves
Australia	$1,977,474.00	Twanna Evans

Logical Processing Order of the SELECT Statement

The results from the previous step will be available to the next step. The logical processing order for a SELECT statement is the following. Actual processing by the database engine may be different due to performance and other considerations.

1. FROM

2.	ON
3.	JOIN
4.	WHERE
5.	GROUP BY
6.	WITH CUBE or WITH ROLLUP
7.	HAVING
8.	SELECT
9.	DISTINCT
10.	ORDER BY
11.	TOP

As an example, it is logical to filter with the WHERE clause prior to applying GROUP BY. It is also logical to sort when the final result set is available.

SELECT Color, COUNT(*) AS ColorCount FROM AdventureWorks2012.Production.Product

WHERE Color is not NULL GROUP BY Color ORDER BY ColorCount DESC;

Color	ColorCount
Black	93
Silver	43
Red	38
Yellow	36
Blue	26
Multi	8
Silver/Black	7
White	4
Grey	1

The TOP Clause

The TOP clause filters results according the sorting specified in an ORDER BY clause, otherwise random filtering takes place.

Simple TOP usage to return 10 rows only.

SELECT TOP 10 SalesOrderID, OrderDate, TotalDue

FROM
AdventureWorks2012.Sales.SalesOrderHeader   ORDER BY TotalDue DESC;

SalesOrderID	OrderDate	TotalDue
51131	2007-07-01 00:00:00.000	187487.825
55282	2007-10-01 00:00:00.000	182018.6272
46616	2006-07-01 00:00:00.000	170512.6689
46981	2006-08-01 00:00:00.000	166537.0808
47395	2006-09-01 00:00:00.000	165028.7482

47369	2006-09-01 00:00:00.000	158056.5449
47355	2006-09-01 00:00:00.000	145741.8553
51822	2007-08-01 00:00:00.000	145454.366
44518	2005-11-01 00:00:00.000	142312.2199
51858	2007-08-01 00:00:00.000	140042.1209

Complex TOP function usage: not known in advance how many rows will be returned due to "TIES".

SELECT   TOP   1   WITH   TIES   coalesce(Color, 'N/A')   AS Color,

            FORMAT(ListPrice,   'c',   'en-US')   AS ListPrice,

        Name
                    AS ProductName,

        ProductID

FROM   AdventureWorks2012.Production.Product

ORDER BY ROW_NUMBER() OVER(PARTITION BY Color ORDER BY ListPrice DESC);

Color	ListPrice	ProductName	ProductID
N/A	$229.49	HL Fork	804
Black	$3,374.99	Mountain-100 Black, 38	775
Red	$3,578.27	Road-150 Red, 62	749
Silver	$3,399.99	Mountain-100 Silver, 38	771
Blue	$2,384.07	Touring-1000 Blue, 46	966
Grey	$125.00	Touring-Panniers, Large	842
Multi	$89.99	Men's Bib-Shorts, S	855
Silver/Black	$80.99	HL Mountain Pedal	937
White	$9.50	Mountain Bike Socks, M	709
Yellow	$2,384.07	Touring-1000 Yellow, 46	954

The DISTINCT Clause to Omit Duplicates

The DISTINCT clause returns only unique results, omitting duplicates in the result set.

USE AdventureWorks2012;

SELECT DISTINCT Color FROM Production.Product

WHERE Color is not NULL

ORDER BY Color;

GO

Color
Black
Blue
Grey
Multi
Red
Silver
Silver/Black
White
Yellow

```
SELECT DISTINCT ListPrice

FROM Production.Product

 WHERE ListPrice > 0.0

ORDER BY ListPrice DESC;

GO

-- (102 row(s) affected) - Partial results.
```

ListPrice
3578.27
3399.99
3374.99
2443.35

```
-- Using DISTINCT in COUNT - NULL is counted

SELECT                     COUNT(*)
            AS TotalRows,

                                    COUNT(DISTINCT
Color)                     AS ProductColors,
```

COUNT(DISTINCT Size) AS ProductSizes

FROM AdventureWorks2012.Production.Product;

TotalRows	ProductColors	ProductSizes
504	9	18

-

The CASE Conditional Expression

The CASE conditional expression evaluates to a single value of the same data type, *therefore* it can be used anywhere in a query where a single value is required.

SELECT   CASE ProductLine

                            WHEN 'R' THEN 'Road'

                            WHEN 'M' THEN 'Mountain'

                            WHEN 'T' THEN 'Touring'

```
                              WHEN 'S' THEN
'Other'

                                   ELSE 'Parts'

                         END
            AS Category,

                    Name
            AS ProductName,

                    ProductNumber

FROM AdventureWorks2012.Production.Product

ORDER BY ProductName;

GO

-- (504 row(s) affected) - Partial results.
```

Category	ProductName	ProductNumber
Touring	Touring-3000 Blue, 62	BK-T18U-62
Touring	Touring-3000 Yellow, 44	BK-T18Y-44
Touring	Touring-3000 Yellow, 50	BK-T18Y-50
Touring	Touring-3000 Yellow, 54	BK-T18Y-54

Touring	Touring-3000 Yellow, 58	BK-T18Y-58
Touring	Touring-3000 Yellow, 62	BK-T18Y-62
Touring	Touring-Panniers, Large	PA-T100
Other	Water Bottle - 30 oz.	WB-H098
Mountain	Women's Mountain Shorts, L	SH-W890-L

Query to return different result sets for repeated execution due to newid().

```
SELECT   TOP 3 CompanyName,   City=CONCAT(City, ', ', Country),          PostalCode,

          [IsNumeric]  =  CASE          WHEN PostalCode like '[0-9][0-9][0-9][0-9][0-9]'

                                        THEN '5-Digit Numeric'   ELSE 'Other'  END

FROM     Northwind.dbo.Suppliers

ORDER BY NEWID();                                --random sort

GO
```

CompanyName	City	PostalCode	IsNumeric
PB Knäckebröd AB	Göteborg, Sweden	S-345 67	Other
Gai pâturage	Annecy, France	74000	5-Digit Numeric
Heli Süßwaren GmbH & Co. KG	Berlin, Germany	10785	5-Digit Numeric

Same query as above expanded with ROW_NUMBER() and another CASE expression column.

```
SELECT          ROW_NUMBER() OVER (ORDER BY
Name)                AS RowNo,

                CASE ProductLine

                    WHEN 'R' THEN 'Road'

                    WHEN 'M' THEN 'Mountain'

                    WHEN 'T' THEN 'Touring'

                    WHEN 'S' THEN 'Other'

                    ELSE 'Parts'

                END
                AS Category,
```

Name

AS ProductName,

CASE WHEN Color is null THEN 'N/A'

ELSE Color

END AS Color,

ProductNumber

FROM Production.Product   ORDER BY ProductName;

-- (504 row(s) affected) - Partial results.

RowNo	Category	ProductName	Color	ProductNumber
1	Parts	Adjustable Race	N/A	AR-5381
2	Mountain	All-Purpose Bike Stand	N/A	ST-1401
3	Other	AWC Logo Cap	Multi	CA-1098
4	Parts	BB Ball Bearing	N/A	BE-2349
5	Parts	Bearing Ball	N/A	BA-8327
6	Other	Bike Wash - Dissolver	N/A	CL-9009

7	Parts	Blade	N/A	BL-2036
8	Other	Cable Lock	N/A	LO-C100
9	Parts	Chain	Silver	CH-0234
10	Parts	Chain Stays	N/A	CS-2812

Testing PostalCode with ISNUMERIC and generating a flag with CASE expression.

SELECT TOP (4)
AddressID,   City,   PostalCode
                 AS Zip,
              CASE WHEN ISNUMERIC(PostalCode) = 1 THEN 'Y' ELSE 'N' END   AS
IsZipNumeric
    FROM   AdventureWorks2008.Person.Address ORDER BY NEWID();

AddressID	City	Zip	IsZipNumeric
16704	Paris	75008	Y
26320	Grossmont	91941	Y
27705	Matraville	2036	Y
18901	Kirkby	KB9	N

The OVER Clause

The OVER clause defines the partitioning and sorting of a rowset (intermediate result set) preceding the application of an associated window function, such as ranking. Window functions are also dubbed as ranking functions.

USE AdventureWorks2012;

-- Query with three different OVER clauses

SELECT   ROW_NUMBER() OVER (ORDER BY SalesOrderID,
ProductID)   AS RowNum

          ,SalesOrderID, ProductID, OrderQty

          ,RANK() OVER(PARTITION BY SalesOrderID ORDER BY OrderQty DESC)   AS Ranking

          ,SUM(OrderQty) OVER(PARTITION BY SalesOrderID)   AS TotalQty

          ,AVG(OrderQty) OVER(PARTITION BY SalesOrderID)   AS AvgQty

```
        ,COUNT(OrderQty) OVER(PARTITION BY
SalesOrderID) AS "Count"  -- T-SQL keyword, use "" or
[]

        ,MIN(OrderQty) OVER(PARTITION BY
SalesOrderID)                              AS
"Min"

        ,MAX(OrderQty) OVER(PARTITION BY
SalesOrderID)                              AS
"Max"

FROM Sales.SalesOrderDetail

WHERE  SalesOrderID  BETWEEN  61190  AND
61199  ORDER BY RowNum;

-- (143 row(s) affected) - Partial results.
```

Row Num	Sales OrderID	Prod uctID	Ord erQty	Ran king	Tot alQty	Av gQty	Co unt	Min	Max
1	61190	707	4	13	159	3	40	1	17
2	61190	708	3	18	159	3	40	1	17
3	61190	711	5	8	159	3	40	1	17
4	61190	712	12	2	159	3	40	1	17
5	61190	714	3	18	159	3	40	1	17
6	61190	715	5	8	159	3	40	1	17
7	61190	716	5	8	159	3	40	1	17
8	61190	858	4	13	159	3	40	1	17
9	61190	859	7	6	159	3	40	1	17

10	61190	864	8	4	159	3	40	1	17
11	61190	865	3	18	159	3	40	1	17
12	61190	870	9	3	159	3	40	1	17
13	61190	876	4	13	159	3	40	1	17
14	61190	877	5	8	159	3	40	1	17
15	61190	880	1	34	159	3	40	1	17
16	61190	881	5	8	159	3	40	1	17
17	61190	883	2	26	159	3	40	1	17
18	61190	884	17	1	159	3	40	1	17
19	61190	885	3	18	159	3	40	1	17

20	61190	886	1	34	159	3	40	1	17
21	61190	889	2	26	159	3	40	1	17
22	61190	892	4	13	159	3	40	1	17
23	61190	893	3	18	159	3	40	1	17
24	61190	895	1	34	159	3	40	1	17

-

FROM Clause: Specifies the Data Source

The FROM clause specifies the source data sets for the query such as tables, views, derived tables and table-valued functions. Typically the tables are JOINed together. The most common JOIN is INNER JOIN which is based on equality between FOREIGN KEY and PRIMARY KEY values in the two tables.

PERFORMANCE NOTE

All FOREIGN KEYs should be indexed. PRIMARY KEYs are indexed automatically with unique index.

```
USE AdventureWorks2012;

GO

SELECT

    ROW_NUMBER()    OVER(ORDER    BY    SalesYTD
DESC)                                        AS
RowNo,

    ROW_NUMBER()  OVER(PARTITION  BY  PostalCode
ORDER BY SalesYTD DESC)            AS SeqNo,

                    CONCAT(p.FirstName,  SPACE(1),
p.LastName)              AS SalesStaff,

                    FORMAT(s.SalesYTD,'c','en-
US')                                        AS
YTDSales,

            City,

            a.PostalCode

                        AS ZipCode

FROM Sales.SalesPerson AS s

  INNER JOIN Person.Person AS p

    ON s.BusinessEntityID = p.BusinessEntityID
```

INNER JOIN Person.Address AS a

ON a.AddressID = p.BusinessEntityID

WHERE   TerritoryID IS NOT NULL   AND
SalesYTD <> 0 ORDER BY ZipCode, SeqNo;

Row No	Seq No	SalesStaff	YTDSales	City	ZipCode
1	1	Linda Mitchell	$4,251,368.55	Issaquah	98027
3	2	Michael Blythe	$3,763,178.18	Issaquah	98027
4	3	Jillian Carson	$3,189,418.37	Issaquah	98027
8	4	Tsvi Reiter	$2,315,185.61	Issaquah	98027
12	5	Garrett Vargas	$1,453,719.47	Issaquah	98027
14	6	Pamela Ansman-Wolfe	$1,352,577.13	Issaquah	98027
2	1	Jae Pak	$4,116,871.23	Renton	98055

5	2	Ranjit Varkey Chudukatil	$3,121,616.32	Renton	98055
6	3	José Saraiva	$2,604,540.72	Renton	98055
7	4	Shu Ito	$2,458,535.62	Renton	98055
9	5	Rachel Valdez	$1,827,066.71	Renton	98055
10	6	Tete Mensa-Annan	$1,576,562.20	Renton	98055
11	7	David Campbell	$1,573,012.94	Renton	98055
13	8	Lynn Tsoflias	$1,421,810.92	Renton	98055

The WHERE Clause to Filter Records (Rows)

The WHERE clause filters the rows generated by the query. Only rows satisfying (TRUE) the WHERE clause predicates are returned.

USE AdventureWorks2012;

String equal match predicate - equal is TRUE, not equal is FALSE.

SELECT ProductID, Name, ListPrice, Color

FROM Production.Product WHERE Name = 'Mountain-100 Silver, 38' ;

ProductID	Name	ListPrice	Color
771	Mountain-100 Silver, 38	3399.99	Silver

-- Function equality predicate

SELECT * FROM Sales.SalesOrderHeader WHERE YEAR(OrderDate) = 2008;

-- (13951 row(s) affected)

```
PERFORMANCE NOTE
When a column is used as a parameter in a function (
e.g. YEAR(OrderDate) ), index (if any) usage is
voided.
Instead of random SEEK, all rows are SCANned in the
table. The predicate is not SARGable.
```

-- String wildcard match predicate

SELECT ProductID, Name, ListPrice, Color

FROM   Production.Product   WHERE   Name   LIKE
('%touring%');

-- Integer range predicate

SELECT ProductID, Name, ListPrice, Color

FROM Production.Product WHERE ProductID >= 997 ;

-- Double string wildcard match predicate

SELECT ProductID, Name, ListPrice, Color

FROM   Production.Product   WHERE   Name   LIKE
('%bike%') AND Name LIKE ('%44%');

-- String list match predicate

SELECT ProductID, Name, ListPrice, Color FROM Production.Product

WHERE Name IN ('Mountain-100 Silver, 44', 'Mountain-100 Black, 44');

The GROUP BY Clause to Aggregate Results

The GROUP BY clause is applied to partition the rows and calculate aggregate values. An extremely powerful way of looking at the data from a summary point of view.

SELECT

V.Name

AS Vendor,

FORMAT(SUM(TotalDue), 'c', 'en-US')

AS TotalPurchase,

A.City,

SP.Name

AS State,

CR.Name

AS Country

FROM Purchasing.Vendor AS V

```
        INNER JOIN Purchasing.VendorAddress AS VA

                    ON VA.VendorID = V.VendorID

        INNER JOIN Person.Address AS A

                    ON A.AddressID = VA.AddressID

        INNER JOIN Person.StateProvince AS SP

                        ON      SP.StateProvinceID
    =   A.StateProvinceID

        INNER JOIN Person.CountryRegion AS CR

                    ON   CR.CountryRegionCode   =
    SP.CountryRegionCode

        INNER JOIN Purchasing.PurchaseOrderHeader POH

                        ON POH.VendorID = V.VendorID

    GROUP BY  V.Name, A.City, SP.Name, CR.Name

    ORDER   BY   SUM(TotalDue)   DESC,   Vendor;     --
    TotalPurchase does a string sort instead of numeric

    GO

    -- (79 row(s) affected) - Partial results.
```

Vendor	TotalPurchase	City	State	Country
Superior Bicycles	$5,034,266.74	Lynnwood	Washington	United States
Professional Athletic Consultants	$3,379,946.32	Burbank	California	United States
Chicago City Saddles	$3,347,165.20	Daly City	California	United States
Jackson Authority	$2,821,333.52	Long Beach	California	United States
Vision Cycles, Inc.	$2,777,684.91	Glendale	California	United States
Sport Fan Co.	$2,675,889.22	Burien	Washington	United States
Proseware, Inc.	$2,593,901.31	Lebanon	Oregon	United States
Crowley Sport	$2,472,770.05	Chicago	Illinois	United States

Greenwood Athletic Company	$2,472,770.05	Lemon Grove	Arizona	United States
Mitchell Sports	$2,424,284.37	Everett	Washington	United States
First Rate Bicycles	$2,304,231.55	La Mesa	New Mexico	United States
Signature Cycles	$2,236,033.80	Coronado	California	United States
Electronic Bike Repair & Supplies	$2,154,773.37	Tacoma	Washington	United States
Vista Road Bikes	$2,090,857.52	Salem	Oregon	United States
Victory Bikes	$2,052,173.62	Issaquah	Washington	United States
Bicycle Specialists	$1,952,375.30	Lake Oswego	Oregon	United States

The HAVING Clause to Filter Aggregates

The HAVING clause is similar to the WHERE clause filtering but applies to GROUP BY aggregates.

USE AdventureWorks;

SELECT

V.Name
AS Vendor,

FORMAT(SUM(TotalDue), 'c', 'en-US')   AS TotalPurchase,

A.City,

SP.Name
AS State,

CR.Name
AS Country

FROM Purchasing.Vendor AS V

INNER JOIN Purchasing.VendorAddress AS VA

ON VA.VendorID = V.VendorID

INNER JOIN Person.Address AS A

ON A.AddressID = VA.AddressID

INNER JOIN Person.StateProvince AS SP

ON   SP.StateProvinceID
=   A.StateProvinceID

INNER JOIN Person.CountryRegion AS CR

ON   CR.CountryRegionCode   =
SP.CountryRegionCode

INNER JOIN Purchasing.PurchaseOrderHeader POH

ON POH.VendorID = V.VendorID

GROUP BY V.Name, A.City, SP.Name, CR.Name

HAVING SUM(TotalDue) < $26000   -- HAVING clause
predicate

ORDER BY SUM(TotalDue) DESC, Vendor;

Vendor	TotalPurchase	City	State	Country
Speed Corporation	$25,732.84	Anacortes	Washington	United

				States
Gardner Touring Cycles	$25,633.64	Altadena	California	United States
National Bike Association	$25,513.90	Sedro Woolley	Washington	United States
Australia Bike Retailer	$25,060.04	Bellingham	Washington	United States
WestAmerica Bicycle Co.	$25,060.04	Houston	Texas	United States
Ready Rentals	$23,635.06	Kirkland	Washington	United States

Morgan Bike Accessories	$23,146.99	Albany	New York	United States
Continental Pro Cycles	$22,960.07	Long Beach	California	United States
American Bicycles and Wheels	$9,641.01	West Covina	California	United States
Litware, Inc.	$8,553.32	Santa Cruz	California	United States
Business Equipment Center	$8,497.80	Everett	Montana	United States

Bloomington Multisport	$8,243.95	West Covina	California	United States
International	$8,061.10	Salt Lake City	Utah	United States
Wide World Importers	$8,025.60	Concord	California	United States
Midwest Sport, Inc.	$7,328.72	Detroit	Michigan	United States
Wood Fitness	$6,947.58	Philadelphia	Pennsylvania	United States
Metro Sport	$6,324.53	Lebanon	Oregon	United d

Equipment				States
Burnett Road Warriors	$5,779.99	Corvallis	Oregon	United States
Lindell	$5,412.57	Lebanon	Oregon	United States
Consumer Cycles	$3,378.17	Torrance	California	United States
Northern Bike Travel	$2,048.42	Anacortes	Washington	United States

Chapter 5: SQL Data Types

In this chapter you will learn the role of data in a database model, how it is defined, its characteristics and the various types that the SQL software supports. There are general data types that are further categorized into different subtypes. It is advisable that you use defined data types to ensure the portability and comprehensibility of the database model.

Data Definition

Data is the stored information in a database that you can manipulate anytime that you want. If you can remember the calling card example in its database model is a collection of customers' names, contact numbers, company addresses, job titles and so on. When rules are provided on how to write and store data, then you need to have a clear understanding of the different *data types*. You need to take into consideration the length or space allocated by the database for every table column and what data values it should contain - whether it is just all letters or all numbers, combination or alphanumeric, graphical, date or time. By defining what data type is stored in each field during the design phase, data entry errors will be prevented. This is the *field definition* process, a form of validation that controls how incorrect data is to be entered into the database.

When a certain database field does not have any data items at all, then the value is unknown or what is called a *null value*. This is completely different from the numeric zero or the blank character value, since zeroes and blanks are still considered definite values. Check out the following scenarios when you might have a null value:

- Even if the data value could possibly exist, you don't know what it is yet.
- The value does not really exist yet.
- The value could be out of range.
- The field is not appropriate for a particular row.

SQL Data Types

These are the general types of SQL data types and their subtypes.

- *Numeric* – The value defined by this data type is either an exact or an approximate number.

- **Exact Numeric**

• *INTEGER* – This consists of positive and negative whole numbers without any decimal nor a fractional part. The INTEGER data value ranges from negative 2,147,483,648 to positive 2,147,483,647, with a maximum storage size of four bytes.

• *SMALLINT* – This replaces integers when you want to save some storage space. However, its precision cannot be larger than that of an integer. Precision in computer programming is the maximum total of significant digits a certain number can have. The SMALLINT data value ranges from negative 32,768 to positive 32,767, with a maximum storage size of two bytes.

• *BIGINT* – This is the reverse of SMALLINT, in which the minimum precision is the same or greater than that of an INTEGER. The BIGINT data value ranges from negative 9,223,372,036,854,775,808 to positive 9,223,372,036,854,775,807, with a maximum storage size of eight bytes.

• *NUMERIC (p, s)* – This data type contains an integer part and a fractional part that indicates the precision and scale of the data value. Scale is the number of digits reserved in the fractional part of the data value (located at the right side of the decimal point). In NUMERIC (p, s), 'p' specifies the precision while 's' specifies the scale. For example, NUMERIC (6, 3) means that the number has a total of 6 significant digits with 3 digits following the decimal point. Therefore, its absolute value will only be up to 999.999.

- *DECIMAL (p, s)* – This also has a fractional component where you can specify both the data value's precision and scale, but allows for greater precision. For example, DECIMAL (6, 3) can contain values up to 999.999 but the database will still accept values larger than 999.999 by rounding off the number. Let us say you entered the number 123.4564, the value that will be stored is 123.456. Thus, the precision given specifies the allocated storage size for this data type.

- **Approximate Numeric**
- *REAL (s)* – This is a single-precision, floating-point number where the decimal point

can "float" within the said number. This gives a limitless precision and a scale of variable lengths for the data type's decimal value. For example, the values for π (pi) can include 3.1, 3.14 and 3.14159 (each value has its own precision). This data type's precision ranges from 1 up to 21, with a maximum storage size of four bytes.

- *DOUBLE PRECISION (p, s)* – As what the name suggests, this is a double-precision, floating-point number with a storage capacity of twice the REAL data type. This data type is suitable when you require more precise numbers, such as in most scientific field of disciplines. This data type's precision ranges from 22 up to 53 digits, with a maximum storage size of eight bytes.

- *FLOAT (p, s)* – This data type lets you specify the value's precision and the computer decides whether it will be a single or a double-precision number. It will allow both the precision of REAL and DOUBLE PRECISION data types. Such features make it easier to move the database from one computer platform to another.

- **String – Considered as the most commonly used data type, this stores alphanumeric information.**
- *CHARACTER (n)* or *CHAR (n)* – Known as a fixed-length string or a constant character, this data type contains strings that have the same length (represented by *'n'*, which is the maximum number of characters allocated for the defined field). For example, setting the column's data type to CHAR (23) means the maximum length of the data to be stored in that field is 23 characters. If its length is less than 23, then the remaining spaces are filled with blanks by SQL. However, this becomes the downside of using fixed-length strings because storage space is totally wasted. On the other hand, if the length is not specified, then SQL assumes a length of just one character. The CHARACTER data type can have a maximum length of 254 characters.

- *CHARACTER VARYING (n)* or *VARCHAR (n)* – This data type is for entries that have different lengths, but the remaining spaces will not be filled by spaces. This means that the exact number of characters entered will be stored in the database to avoid space wastage. The maximum length for this data type is 32,672 characters with no default value.

• *CHARACTER LARGE OBJECT (CLOB)* – This was introduced in SQL:1999 where the variable-length data type is used, which contains a Unicode, character-based information. Such data is too big to be stored as a CHARACTER type, just like large documents, and the maximum value is up to 2,147,483,647 characters long.

• **Date and Time – This data type handles information associated with dates and times.**

• *DATE* – This provides a storage space for the date's year, month and day values (in that particular order). The value for the year is expressed in four digits (represented by values ranging from 0001 up to 9999), while the month and day values are both represented by any two digits. The format of this data type is: *'yyyy-mm-dd.'*

- *TIME* – This stores and displays time values using an hour-minute-second format (*"HH:MM:SS"*).

- *DATETIME* – This contains both date and time information displayed using the "YYYY-MM-DD HH:MM:SS" format. The range of this data type is from "1000-01-01 00:00:00" to "9999-12-31 23:59:59".

- *TIMESTAMP* – Similar to the DATETIME data type, this ranges from "1970-01-01 00:00:01" UTC to "2038-01-19 03:14:07" UTC.

- *Boolean* – This data type is used for comparing information and based from the results they can return TRUE, FALSE, or NULL values. If all the conditions for a given query are met, then Boolean value returns TRUE. Otherwise, the value is either FALSE or NULL.

User-Defined Data Type

We will now discuss user-defined data types or simply UDT's. By the name itself, the user defines or specifies the data values based on the existing data types. This allows customization to meet other user requirements and maximize the available storage space. Moreover, programmers enjoy the flexibility they bring in developing database applications. UDT's make it possible when you need to store the same type of data in a column that will also be defined in several tables. The CREATE TYPE statement is used to define UDT's.

For example, if you need to use two different currencies for your database like the US dollar and the UK pound, you can create and define the following UDT's:

CREATE TYPE USDollar AS DECIMAL (9, 2) ;

CREATE TYPE UKPound AS DECIMAL (9, 2) ;

- Data is the stored information in a database that a user can define and manipulate.
- There are different general SQL data types, namely numeric, string, date and time, and Boolean.
- If you want to define more specific data types when designing your database model, you can use the different subtypes under each general SQL data type.
- UDT's or user-defined data types are customized and created by the user based on

the existing data types, which gives flexibility in developing various database applications.

In the next chapter you will learn the common SQL commands that are used to create, manipulate and retrieve data from a database, in an efficient and effective way.

Chapter 6: Cursors: Read Only, Forward Only, Fast Forward, Static, Scroll, Dynamic, Optimistic

Cursors are database objects that are used to iterate over a set of rows and generally perform some additional logical operations or others on each row of fetched data. The process of cursor operation entails following tasks:

a. *Declare the variables to be used*

b. *Define the Cursor and type of cursor*

c. *Populate Cursor with values using SELECT*

d. *Open Cursor that was declared & populated above*

e. Fetch the values from Cursor in to declared variables

f. *While loop to fetch next row and loop till no longer rows exist*

g. Perform any data processing on that row inside while loop

h. *Close Cursor to gracefully un-lock tables in any*

i. *Remove Cursor from memory*

However, Cursors are generally not recommended due to row-by-row fetching and processing of data, consumption of memory (due to allocation of temporary table and filling it with the result set) and sometimes locking tables in unpredictable ways. Thus, alternate approaches like using *while* loop needs to be considered before using cursors.

LOCAL/GLOBAL CURSOR

This cursor specifies the scope and whether this scope allows locally to a stored procedure or trigger or even a batch OR if the scope of the cursor is applicable globally for the connection. Cursor is valid only within the scope defined.

FORWARD_ONLY CURSOR

FORWARD_ONLY Cursor specifies that rows can only be scrolled from first to the end row. Thus, this precludes moving to *prior* or *last* row and *fetch next* is only option available. Below is an example of *FORWARD_ONLY Cursor*:

```
--
==================================
-- Author:        Neal Gupta
```

-- Create date: 12/01/2013

-- Description: Create a Cursor for displaying customer info

--

==================================

DECLARE

        @CustomerID INT

       ,@FirstName VARCHAR(50)

  ,@LastName VARCHAR(50)

      ,@City VARCHAR(50)

      ,@State VARCHAR(10)

      ,@ZipCode VARCHAR(10)

-- Create a Cursor

DECLARE curTblCustomer CURSOR FORWARD_ONLY

FOR

SELECT

      CustomerID, FirstName, LastName, City, [State], ZipCode

FROM [IMS].[dbo].[TblCustomer]

```
ORDER BY CustomerID ASC;

-- Open the Cursor

OPEN curTblCustomer

-- Get the first Customer

FETCH NEXT FROM curTblCustomer INTO @CustomerID,
@FirstName, @LastName, @City, @State,@ZipCode

PRINT 'Customer Details:'

-- Loop thru all the customers

WHILE @@FETCH_STATUS = 0

        BEGIN

            -- Display customer details

        PRINT CAST(@CustomerID AS VARCHAR(50)) +
        ' ' + @FirstName + ' ' + @LastName + '
        '+ @City + ' '+ @State + ' '+ @ZipCode
            -- Get the next customer

        FETCH NEXT FROM curTblCustomer INTO
        @CustomerID, @FirstName, @LastName,
        @City, @State, @ZipCode
END

-- Close Cursor
```

CLOSE curTblCustomer

-- Remove Cursor from memory of temp database

DEALLOCATE curTblCustomer

Cursor by default is FORWARD_ONLY, if *STATIC, KEYSET* or *DYNAMIC* options are not mentioned and cursor works as a *DYNAMIC* one if these 3 keywords are not specified.

READ_ONLY CURSOR

This cursor is similar to above *FORWARD_ONLY* cursor, except that updates on the current fetched row cannot be performed.

FAST_FORWARD CURSOR

This cursor is really a combination of *FAST_FORWARD* (#1) and *READ_ONLY* (#2) along with performance optimizations. Since, it is a *fast forward* cursor, it precludes scrolling to prior or last row and being *read only* cursor also, prevents update of current fetched row. However, due to these 2 restrictions, they help SQL server to optimize the overall cursor performance.

--

===================================

```
-- Description: Create a FAST_FORWARD Cursor
===================================
DECLARE

        @CustomerID INT

        ,@FirstName VARCHAR(50)

    ,@LastName VARCHAR(50)

        ,@City VARCHAR(50)

        ,@State VARCHAR(10)

        ,@ZipCode VARCHAR(10)

-- Create a Cursor

DECLARE curTblCustomer CURSOR FAST_FORWARD

FOR

SELECT

        CustomerID

    ,FirstName
    ,LastName
    ,City
    ,[State]
    ,ZipCode
FROM
```

[IMS].[dbo].[TblCustomer]

```
ORDER BY

        CustomerID ASC;

-- Open the Cursor

OPEN curTblCustomer

-- Get the first Customer

FETCH NEXT FROM curTblCustomer INTO @CustomerID,
@FirstName, @LastName, @City, @State, @ZipCode

PRINT 'Customer Details:'

-- Loop thru all the customers

WHILE @@FETCH_STATUS = 0

        BEGIN

            -- Display customer details

        PRINT CAST(@CustomerID AS VARCHAR(50)) +
        ' ' + @FirstName + ' ' + @LastName + '
        '+ @City + ' '+ @State + ' '+ @ZipCode
            -- Get the next customer

        FETCH NEXT FROM curTblCustomer INTO
        @CustomerID, @FirstName, @LastName,
        @City, @State, @ZipCode
END
```

-- Close Cursor

CLOSE curTblCustomer

-- Remove Cursor from memory of temp database

DEALLOCATE curTblCustomer

STATIC CURSOR

If a cursor is specified as *STATIC*, SQL server takes a snapshot of the data and places into temporary table in *tempdb* database. So, when the cursor fetches next row, data comes from this temporary table and therefore, if something is modified in the original table, it is not reflected in the temporary table. This makes the performance of cursor faster as compared to dynamic cursor (explained below) since next row of data is already pre-fetched in temp database.

DYNAMIC CURSOR

As the name suggests, when the cursor is scrolling to next row, data for that row is dynamically brought from the original table, and if there was any change, it is reflected in the data fetched as well.

SCROLL CURSOR

This cursor allows scrolling of rows: *FIRST, LAST, PRIOR, NEXT* and if a cursor is not specified as SCROLL, it can only perform *FETCH* next row. If the cursor is *FAST_FORWARD, SCROLL* option cannot be used.

OPTIMISTIC/SCROLL_LOCKS CURSOR

Below is a cursor declaration using some of the above options: *LOCAL, FORWARD_ONLY, STATIC and READ_ONLY*:

DECLARE curTblCustomerOp1 CURSOR

    LOCAL

    FORWARD_ONLY

    STATIC

    READ_ONLY

FOR

-- Rest of SQL remains same as used in FORWARD_ONLY Cursor

Another cursor declaration could use following options: *GLOBAL, SCROLL, DYNAMIC, OPTIMISTIC:*

DECLARE curTblCustomerOp2 CURSOR

GLOBAL   -- OR USE LOCAL

SCROLL   -- OR USE FORWARD_ONLY

DYNAMIC   --   OR   USE
FAST_FORWARD/STATIC/KEYSET

OPTIMISTIC -- OR USE READ_ONLY/SCROLL_LOCKS

FOR

-- Rest of SQL remains same as used in FORWARD_ONLY Cursor

NESTED CURSOR

As the name suggest, cursors can be nested, meaning one cursor can have another inner cursor and so on. In below example we will use one nested cursor.

--

===================================

-- Description: Create a Nested Cursor for displaying Orders

-- and products ordered

--

===================================

```
DECLARE

        @OrderID INT

        ,@ProductID INT

        ,@OrderQty INT

        ,@OrderDate DATETIME

        ,@Name VARCHAR(50)

        ,@Manufacturer VARCHAR(50)

        ,@Price DECIMAL(9,2)

PRINT '***** Orders Details *****'

--- First, declare OUTER Cursor

DECLARE curTblOrder CURSOR

        LOCAL

    FORWARD  ONLY

    STATIC

        READ  ONLY

    TYPE  WARNING

FOR

        SELECT
```

```sql
            OrderID

            ,ProductID

            ,OrderQty

            ,OrderDate

      FROM

            [IMS].[dbo].[TblOrder]

      ORDER BY

            OrderID

-- Open OUTER Cursor

OPEN curTblOrder

-- Fetch data from cursor and populate into variables

FETCH NEXT FROM curTblOrder INTO @OrderID,
@ProductID, @OrderQty, @OrderDate

WHILE @@FETCH_STATUS = 0

BEGIN

      PRINT '*** Order: ' + ' ' + CAST(@OrderID AS
VARCHAR(10))

   -- Now, declare INNER Cursor

   DECLARE curTblProduct CURSOR
```

```
FOR

        SELECT Name, Manufacturer, Price

        FROM [IMS].[dbo].[TblProduct] P

        WHERE P.ProductID = @ProductID


    -- Open INNER Cursor
OPEN curTblProduct

FETCH NEXT FROM curTblProduct INTO @Name,
@Manufacturer, @Price

        -- Loop for INNER Cursor
WHILE @@FETCH_STATUS = 0
BEGIN
PRINT 'Product: ' + @Name + ' ' + @Manufacturer + ' '
+ CAST(@Price AS VARCHAR(15))

        FETCH NEXT FROM curTblProduct INTO
@Name, @Manufacturer, @Price

    END
    -- Close INNER Cursor first and deallocate it
from temp database
CLOSE curTblProduct
```

DEALLOCATE curTblProduct

-- Fetch next Order

FETCH NEXT FROM **curTblOrder** INTO **@OrderID**, **@ProductID**, **@OrderQty**, @OrderDate

END

-- Finally, close OUTER Cursor and deallocate it from temp database

CLOSE curTblOrder

DEALLOCATE curTblOrder

FOR UPDATE CURSOR

This cursor allows updating the column values in the fetched row for the specified columns only, however, if the columns are not specified, then, all the columns can be updated for the row under consideration using *WHERE CURRENT OF* clause.

ALTERNATIVE APPROACH

Note that in above examples, we used cursors to demonstrate the functionality of different types of cursor, however, we could have used alternative approach, like using *WHILE* loop and *counter*

approach to perform similar task, as was done in #2 above, as below:

```
--
================================
-- Description: Alternative Approach
-- using WHILE loop and Counter Method
--
================================
    DECLARE @Customers TABLE
      RowID INT IDENTITY(1,1) PRIMARY KEY
      ,CustomerID INT
      ,FirstName VARCHAR(50)
      ,LastName VARCHAR(50)
      ,City VARCHAR(50)
      ,[State] VARCHAR(25)
      ,ZipCode VARCHAR(10)
    DECLARE
        @StartCount INT = 1        -- First Row
Count
```

```
        ,@EndCount INT                         -- Total
Row Counts

            ,@CustomerID INT

            ,@FirstName VARCHAR(50)

            ,@LastName VARCHAR(50)

            ,@City VARCHAR(50)

            ,@State VARCHAR(50)

            ,@ZipCode VARCHAR(10)
-- Bulk Insert all the customers into temp table:
@Customers

    INSERT          INTO          @Customers
(CustomerID,FirstName,LastName,City,[State],ZipCode
)

    SELECT

        CustomerID

            ,FirstName

            ,LastName

            ,City

            ,[State]

            ,ZipCode
```

```sql
    FROM
                    [IMS].[dbo].[TblCustomer]      WITH
(NOLOCK)
-- EndCount is set to total of all rows fetched in above
SELECT
    SELECT @EndCount = @@ROWCOUNT
-- Loop thru all the rows
    WHILE @StartCount <= @EndCount
BEGIN
            SELECT
                    @CustomerID = CustomerID
                    ,@FirstName = FirstName
                    ,@LastName = LastName
                    ,@City = City
                    ,@State = [State]
                    ,@ZipCode = ZipCode
            FROM @Customers
            WHERE
                    RowID = @StartCount
```

```
PRINT 'Fetched Row#: ' + CAST(@StartCount AS
VARCHAR(5)) + ' from TblCustomer table. Details below:
'

                    PRINT 'CustomerID  =  '+
CAST(@CustomerID AS VARCHAR(5)) + '

            FirstName = ' + @FirstName + '
LastName = ' + @LastName + ' City

            = ' + @City + ' State = ' + @State
+ ' ZipCode = ' + @ZipCode

        SELECT @StartCount += 1

END
```

Chapter 7: Preparation

To successfully connect to and work with a SQL Server Database from your Windows PC (desktop or notebook), there are several things that must be properly setup or configured. None of these are very complex, but failure to address these items can and will result in either problems, warnings and/or errors. So while this chapter may be brief, the basic concepts (and their mental images) are nonetheless very critical for your success. So it would be wise to read and learn this chapter's material well.

Database Architecture

The SQL Server database itself will most often reside upon a server somewhere within your organization. While you can both run and access the SQL Server database on most PC's these days, the raw performance, tight security and high availability requirements alone generally require a secure, centrally managed database server.

Database Architecture

The critical item of note is that both the client and the server need some supporting SQL Server network library files in order for communication between your application and the database to occur. Because it's not necessary to know anything about TDS to connect to a SQL Server database, we won't delve any further into the specifics about it.

What is important is you must have those network library files on your PC for database connections to function properly. Since Windows 2000, all versions of Windows have at least a basic set of these network library files already pre-installed. SQL Server 2005 introduced a new set of network files called the SQL Server Native Client which provides additional functionality based on new features that was added to that version of SQL Server. The features are not essential to retrieve data from a SQL Server database but center around security and management functionality such as the ability to handle passwords similar to the way Windows does. However, if you don't use these additional features, chances are you already have everything you need to connect to the SQL Server database.

Database Versions

The SQL Server database, like most software, has different versions – such as SQL Server 2000, 2005,

2008, and 2008 R2. These are simply the marketing names for the initial or base releases. In addition there are numerous patches available, usually called service packs or cumulative updates. If you're experiencing an issue with something not working the way you'd expect it to, you might check with your system administrator or database administrator to see if one of these is needed. But typically they are only required if you installed specific client software from the SQL Server CDs/DVDs.

Connecting

Thus far we've primarily covered terminology and that is a prerequisite for successfully working with your SQL Server databases. Now it's time to perform your very first SQL Server database task – connecting to your database. That may seem like an anticlimactic task but it's the first step in making use of the data within those databases.

Think of creating the database connection like making a phone call. If you don't have the proper equipment, a service plan, the number of whom you're calling and knowledge of how to dial that number, then you cannot initiate a phone call and thus cannot hold a meaningful conversation. The same is true for databases. You must successfully connect before you can retrieve, insert or update your data.

Connecting Via ODBC

A lot of applications connect to SQL Server using a method called ODBC. Either the application will present an interface where you can create your connection or it will ask you for an existing ODBC connection. Chances are that if it presents an interface, the steps will be similar to when you create your own ODBC connection. In fact, a lot of times applications will simply re-use Windows' own tool for managing these connections. So let's look at how to do that.

Control Panel icon

You'll want to click on it and that will bring up the Control Panel. If you're in Classic View, you should see an icon for Administrative Tools. If you're in Category View you'll have to double-click on the Performance and Maintenance icon first. Once you see the Administrative Tools icon, double-click on it and you should have a new list of options. What you're looking for is the icon for Data Sources (ODBC). Double-click on it and it will bring up the tool ODBC Administrator where you'll be able to configure a new ODBC connection.

There are two types of data sources called data set names (i.e. DSN): user and system. User ones can only be seen and used by the current Windows user, whereas system ones can be seen and used by any Windows user on that same PC.

ODBC Admin Main Screen

Here we have a good number of choices, but usually you'll just want the one that says SQL Server. In this example, the full SQL Server tools are installed for several versions of SQL Server, which is why you also see choices for SQL Server Native Client. You likely won't have the SQL Server Native Client choices unless you need them. Simply select SQL Server and click Finish.

SQL Server Data Source

In the event that you'll one day need to connect to a different database server (Oracle, DB2, etc.) generally speaking you will have the most reliable results and fastest performance using the ODBC driver from the database vendor and it likely will be named so you easily recognize it.

Choose the Name and SQL Server

You'll then need to choose how you connect to the SQL Server in the sense of how does SQL Server know who you are. Most of the time, you'll connect using the user account you logged on to Windows with. If you need a special SQL Server login, your system or database administrator should provide it ahead of time, along with the appropriate password. In either case, make the appropriate selections for the next screen,

Tell SQL Server Who You Are

Next, you'll need to specify any other options for the connection. Here you'll want to check the checkbox to change the default database and then choose the right one from the drop down list. If you should get an error here, it means either the SQL Server you specified in the previous screen is not available, or you mistyped its name, or you don't have permission to connect. If that's the case, go back to the previous screen, check the name of the SQL Server, and if you believe it's right, follow up with your system or database administrator. It could be down or there could be another reason as to why you can't connect to it.

Specify the Database

This is the database I know contains the sales information I want to access. You'll need to know both the server and the database name to get at the data stored on the SQL Server.

Click the Next button to go to the last configuration screen, where you likely won't need to make any changes, then click Finish to create your ODBC connection. You should be presented with a screen like in - be sure to test your connection to make sure everything is fine before clicking OK.

Review Setup

Conclusion

In this chapter we reviewed the basic concepts and processes you need to understand and perform in order to begin successfully working with your SQL Server databases. We also reviewed covered the prerequisite knowledge to tackle the first and most critical database task – connecting. Much like a phone call – we entered the information necessary to dial in to the database and then placed the call.

Chapter 8: Filters

WHERE Clause

WHERE is the most widely used clause. It helps retrieve exactly what you require. The following example table displays the STUDENT STRENGTH in various Engineering courses in a college:

ENGINEERING_STUDENTS

ENGG_ID	ENGG_NAME	STUDENT_STRENGTH
1	Electronics	150
2	Software	250
3	Genetic	75
4	Mechanical	150
5	Biomedical	72
6	Instrumentation	80
7	Chemical	75

8	Civil	60
9	Electronics & Com	250
10	Electrical	60

Now, if you want to know how many courses have over 200 in STUDENT STRENGTH, then you can simplify your search by passing on a simple statement:

SELECT ENGG_NAME, STUDENT_STRENGTH

FROM ENGINEERING_STUDENTS

WHERE STUDENT_STRENGTH > 200;

ENGG_NAME	STUDENT_STRENGTH
Software	250
Electronics & Com	250

HAVING Clause

HAVING is another clause used as a filter in SQL. At this point, it is important to understand the difference between the WHERE and HAVING clauses. WHERE specifies a condition, and only that set of data that passes the condition will be fetched and displayed in the result set. HAVING clause is used to filter grouped or summarized data. If a SELECT query has both WHERE and HAVING clauses, then when WHERE is used to filter rows, the result is aggregated so the HAVING clause can be applied. You will get a better understanding when you see an example.

For an explanation, another table by the name of Dept_Data has been created, and it is defined as follows:

Field	Type	Null	Key	Default	Extra
Dept_ ID	Bigint (20)	NO	PRI	NULL	auto_ increment
HOD	Varchar (35)	NO			
NO_	Varchar	YES		NULL	

OF_ Prof	(35)				
ENGG_ ID	Smallint (6)	YES	MUL	NULL	

Now, let's have a look at the data available in this table:

Where Dept_ID is set to 100.

Dept_ID	HOD	NO_OF_Prof	ENGG_ID
100	Miley Andrews	7	1
101	Alex Dawson	6	2
102	Victoria Fox	7	3
103	Anne Joseph	5	4
104	Sophia Williams	8	5
105	Olive Brown	4	6

106	Joshua Taylor	6	7
107	Ethan Thomas	5	8
108	Michael Anderson	8	9
109	Martin Jones	5	10

There are a few simple differences between the WHERE and HAVING clauses. The WHERE clause can be used with SELECT, UPDATE, and DELETE clauses, but the HAVING clause does not enjoy that privilege; it is only used in the SELECT query. The WHERE clause can be used for individual rows, but HAVING is applied on grouped data. If the WHERE and HAVING clauses are used together, then the WHERE clause will be used before the GROUP BY clause, and the HAVING clause will be used after the GROUP BY clause. Whenever WHERE and HAVING clauses are used together in a query, the WHERE clause is applied first on every row to filter the results and ensure a group is created. After that, you will apply the HAVING clause on that group.

Now, based on our previous tables, let's see which departments have more than 5 professors:

SELECT * FROM Dept_Data WHERE NO_OF_Prof > 5;

Look at the WHERE clause here. It will check each and every row to see which record has NO_OF_Prof > 5.

Dept_ID	HOD	NO_OF_Prof	ENGG_ID
100	Miley Andrews	7	1
101	Alex Dawson	6	2
102	Victoria Fox	7	3
104	Sophia Williams	8	5
106	Joshua Taylor	6	7
108	Michael Anderson	8	9

Now, let's find the names of the Engineering courses for the above data:

SELECT e. ENGG_NAME, e.STUDENT_STRENGTH,

d.HOD,d.NO_OF_Prof,d.Dept_ID

FROM ENGINEERING_STUDENTS e, Dept_Data d

WHERE d.NO_OF_Prof > 5

AND e.ENGG_ID = d.ENGG_ID;

The result set will be as follows:

ENGG_NAME	STUDENT_ STRENGTH	HOD	NO_ OF_ Prof	Dept_ID
Electronics	150	Miley Andrews	7	100
Software	250	Alex Dawson	6	101
Genetic	75	Victoria Fox	7	102
Biomedical	72	Sophia Williams	8	104

Chemical	75	Joshua Taylor	6	106
Electronics & Com	250	Michael Anderson	8	108

Next, we GROUP the data as shown below:

SELECT   e.ENGG_NAME, d.HOD,d.NO_OF_Prof,d.Dept_ID

FROM ENGINEERING_STUDENTS e, Dept_Data d

WHERE   d.NO_OF_Prof > 5 AND e.ENGG_ID = d.ENGG_ID

GROUP BY ENGG_NAME;

ENGG_NAME	STUDENT_ STRENGTH	HOD	NO_ OF_ Prof	Dept_ID
Biomedical	72	Sophia Williams	8	104
Chemical	75	Joshua Taylor	6	106
Electronics	150	Miley Andrews	7	100

Electronics & Com	250	Michael Anderson	8	108
Genetic	75	Victoria Fox	7	102
Software	250	Alex Dawson	6	101

Let's see which departments from this group have more than 100 students:

SELECT e. ENGG_NAME, e.STUDENT_STRENGTH,

d.HOD,d.NO_OF_Prof,d.Dept_ID

FROM ENGINEERING_STUDENTS e, Dept_Data d

WHERE d.NO_OF_Prof > 5 AND e.ENGG_ID = d.ENGG_ID
GROUP BY e.ENGG_NAME HAVING e.STUDENT_STRENGTH > 100;

ENGG_NAME	STUDENT_STRENGTH	HOD	NO_OF_Prof	Dept_ID
Electronics	150	Miley Andrews	7	100
Electronics & Com	250	Michael Anderson	8	108
Software	250	Alex Dawson	6	101

Evaluating a Condition

A WHERE clause can evaluate more than one condition where every condition is separated by the AND operator. Let's take a look at the example below:

SELECT e. ENGG_NAME, e.STUDENT_STRENGTH,

d.HOD,d.NO_OF_Prof,d.Dept_ID

FROM ENGINEERING_STUDENTS e, Dept_Data d

WHERE d.NO_OF_Prof > 5 AND

e.ENGG_ID = d.ENGG_ID AND

100 < e.STUDENT_STRENGTH < 250;

ENGG_NAME	STUDENT_ STRENGTH	HOD	NO_OF_ Prof	Dept_ ID
Electronics	150	Miley Andrews	7	100
Software	250	Alex Dawson	6	101
Genetic	75	Victoria Fox	7	102
Biomedical	72	Sophia Williams	8	104
Chemical	75	Joshua Taylor	6	106
Electronics & Com	250	Michael Anderson	8	108

There is one thing you must understand with the WHERE clause. It is only when all conditions become true for a row that it is included in the result set. If even one condition turns out to be false, the row will not be included in the result set.

The result set will be different if you replace any or all AND operators in the above statement with the OR operator. Say you need to find out which department has either fewer than 100 students OR fewer than 5 professors. Have a look at the following statement:

SELECT e. ENGG_NAME,e.STUDENT_STRENGTH,

d.HOD,d.NO_OF_Prof,d.Dept_ID,e.ENGG_ID

FROM ENGINEERING_STUDENTS e, Dept_Data d

WHERE e.ENGG_ID = d.ENGG_ID AND

(e.STUDENT_STRENGTH < 100 OR d.NO_OF_Prof < 5);

ENGG_NAME	STUDENT _STRENGTH	HOD	NO_ OF_ Prof	Dept_ ID
Genetic	75	Victoria Fox	7	102
Biomedical	72	Sophia Williams	8	104
Instrumentation	80	Olive Brown	4	105
Chemical	75	Joshua Taylor	6	106
Civil	60	Ethan Thomas	5	107
Electrical	60	Martin Jones	5	109

In the above statement, notice how the parentheses are placed. You should clearly define how the AND operator exists between two conditions, and how the OR operator exists between two conditions. You will learn more about the usage of parentheses in the upcoming section. For now, please understand how the outcome of the AND/OR operators are evaluated.

AND Operator

Condition	Outcome
Where True AND True	True
Where False AND True	False
Where True AND False	False
Where False AND False	False

OR Operator

Condition	Outcome
Where True OR True	True
Where False OR True	True
Where True OR False	True
Where False OR False	False

Usage of Parentheses

In the last example, we had three conditions, and we put one condition in parentheses. If the parentheses are missing, the results will be wrong and confusing. For a change, let's try and see what happens if this occurs:

SELECT e.ENGG_NAME,e.STUDENT_STRENGTH,

d.HOD,d.NO_OF_Prof,d.Dept_ID,e.ENGG_ID

FROM ENGINEERING_STUDENTS e, DEPT_DATA d

WHERE e.ENGG_ID = d.ENGG_ID AND

e.STUDENT_STRENGTH < 100 OR d.NO_OF_Prof < 5;

ENGG_ NAME	STUDEN T_ STRENG TH	HOD	NO _ OF _ Pro f	Dept_ ID	ENGG_ ID
Genetic	75	Victori a Fox	7	102	3

Biomedical	72	Sophia Williams	8	104	5
Electronics	150	Olive Brown	4	105	1
Software	250	Olive Brown	4	105	2
Genetic	75	Olive Brown	4	105	3
Mechanical	150	Olive Brown	4	105	4
Biomedical	72	Olive Brown	4	105	5
Instrumentation	80	Olive Brown	4	105	6
Chemical	75	Olive Brown	4	105	7

Civil	60	Olive Brown	4	105	8
Electronics & Com	250	Olive Brown	4	105	9
Electrical	60	Olive Brown	4	105	10
Chemical	75	Joshua Taylor	6	106	7
Civil	60	Ethan Thomas	5	107	8
Electrical	60	Martin Jones	5	109	10

One look at the table above and you know the results are all wrong and misleading. The reason is that the instructions are not clear to the data server. Now, think about what we want to accomplish; we want to know which department has fewer than 100 students OR fewer than 5 professors. Now, witness the magic of the parentheses. The parentheses convert three conditions to two, well-defined conditions.

WHERE e.ENGG_ID = d.ENGG_ID AND

(e.STUDENT_STRENGTH < 100 OR d.NO_OF_Prof < 5);

This follows the following format: Condition1 AND (Condition2 OR Condition3).

Now, this is how the condition will be calculated:

Cond1	Cond2	Cond3	Cond2 OR Cond3	Cond1 AND (Cond2 OR Cond3)
T	T	T	T	T
T	T	F	T	T
T	F	T	T	T
T	F	F	F	F
F	T	T	T	F

F	T	F	T	F
F	F	T	T	F
F	F	F	F	F

By putting e.STUDENT_STRENGTH < 100 OR d.NO_OF_Prof < 5 into parentheses, we convert it into one condition, and the first condition will consider the output of the parentheses for the final result. Out of eight possible conditions from the table above, there are only three scenarios where the final condition is True.

The NOT Operator

To understand the usage of the NOT operator, let's replace AND with AND NOT and find out what output we receive:

SELECT e. ENGG_NAME,e.STUDENT_STRENGTH,

d.HOD,d.NO_OF_Prof,d.Dept_ID,e.ENGG_ID

FROM ENGINEERING_STUDENTS e, Dept_Data d

WHERE e.ENGG_ID = d.ENGG_ID AND NOT

(e.STUDENT_STRENGTH < 100 OR d.NO_OF_Prof < 5);

ENGG_ NAME	STUDENT_ STRENGTH	HOD	NO_ OF_ Prof	Dept_ ID	ENGG_ ID
Electronics	150	Miley Andrews	7	100	1
Software	250	Alex Dawson	6	101	2
Mechanical	150	Anne Joseph	5	103	4
Electronics & Com	250	Michael Anderson	8	108	9

Remember that our desired results find which department has fewer than 100 students or fewer than 5 professors. After applying the NOT operator before the parentheses, our results look for either more than 5 professors, or more than 100 students.

Is it possible to obtain the same results while using the NOT statement? Yes! Just replace '>' with '<' and replace OR with AND.

SELECT e.ENGG_NAME,e.STUDENT_STRENGTH,

d.HOD,d.NO_OF_Prof,d.Dept_ID,e.ENGG_ID

FROM ENGINEERING_STUDENTS e, Dept_Data d

WHERE e.ENGG_ID = d.ENGG_ID AND NOT

(e.STUDENT_STRENGTH ≥ 100 AND d.NO_OF_Prof ≥ 5);

ENGG_NAME	STUDENT_STRENGTH	HOD	NO_OF_Prof	Dept_ID	ENGG_ID
Genetic	75	Victoria Fox	7	102	3
Biomedical	72	Sophia Williams	8	104	5
Instrumentation	80	Olive Brown	4	105	6
Chemical	75	Joshua Taylor	6	106	7
Civil	60	Ethan Thomas	5	107	8
Electrical	60	Martin Jones	5	109	10

Here is the output for applying AND NOT:

Cond1	Cond2	Cond3	Cond2 AND Cond3	Cond1 AND NOT (Cond2 AND Cond3)
T	T	T	T	F
T	T	F	F	T
T	F	T	F	T
T	F	F	F	T
F	T	T	T	T
F	T	F	F	T
F	F	T	F	T
F	F	F	F	T

However, use the NOT operator only when required. It can aid in the legibility of the statement, but if you use

NOT when it can be avoided, it could unnecessarily complicate things for the developer.

Sequences

A sequence refers to a set of numbers that has been generated in a specified order on demand. These are popular in databases. The reason behind this is that sequences provide an easy way to have a unique value for each row in a specified column. This section explains the use of sequences in SQL.

AUTO_INCREMENT Column

This provides you with the easiest way of creating a sequence in MySQL. You only have to define the column as auto_increment and leave MySQL to take care of the rest. To show how to use this property, we will create a simple table and insert some records into the table.

The following command will help us create the table:

CREATE TABLE colleagues

(

id INT UNSIGNED NOT NULL AUTO_INCREMENT,

PRIMARY KEY (id),

name VARCHAR(20) NOT NULL,

home_city VARCHAR(20) NOT NULL

);

The command should create the table successfully, as shown below:

```
mysql> create database tuw
    -> ;
Query OK, 1 row affected (0.05 sec)

mysql> use tuw;
Database changed
mysql> CREATE TABLE colleagues
    ->    (
    ->    id INT UNSIGNED NOT NULL AUTO_INCREMENT,
    ->    PRIMARY KEY (id),
    ->    name VARCHAR(20) NOT NULL,
    ->    home_city VARCHAR(20) NOT NULL
    -> );
Query OK, 0 rows affected (0.30 sec)

mysql>
```

We have created a table named colleagues. This table has 3 columns: id, name, and home_city. The first column is an integer data type while the rest are varchars (variable characters). We have added the auto_increment property to the id column, so the column values will be incremented automatically. When entering data into the table, we don't need to specify the value of this column. It will start at 1 by default then increment the values automatically for each record you insert into the table.

Let us now insert some records into the table:

INSERT INTO colleagues

VALUES (NULL, "John", "New Delhi");

INSERT INTO colleagues

VALUES (NULL, "Joel", "New Jersey");

INSERT INTO colleagues

VALUES (NULL, "Britney", "New York");

INSERT INTO colleagues

VALUES (NULL, "Biggy", "Washington");

The commands should run successfully, as shown below:

Now, we can run the select statement against the table and see its contents:

```
mysql> select * from colleagues;
+----+---------+-------------+
| id | name    | home_city   |
+----+---------+-------------+
|  1 | John    | New Delhi   |
|  2 | Joel    | New Jersey  |
|  3 | Britney | New York    |
|  4 | Biggy   | Washington  |
+----+---------+-------------+
4 rows in set (0.01 sec)

mysql>
```

We see that the id column has also been populated with values starting from 1. Each time you enter a record, the value of this column is increased by 1. We have successfully created a sequence.

Renumbering a Sequence

You notice that when you delete a record from a sequence such as the one we have created above, the records will not be renumbered. You may not be impressed by this kind of numbering. However, it is possible for you to re-sequence the records. This only involves a single trick, but make sure to check whether the table has a join with another table or not.

If you find you have to re-sequence your records, the best way to do it is by dropping the column and then adding it. Here, we'll show how to drop the id column of the colleagues table.

The table is as follows for now:

```
mysql> select * from colleagues;
+----+---------+-------------+
| id | name    | home_city   |
+----+---------+-------------+
|  1 | John    | New Delhi   |
|  2 | Joel    | New Jersey  |
|  3 | Britney | New York    |
|  4 | Biggy   | Washington  |
+----+---------+-------------+
4 rows in set (0.01 sec)

mysql>
```

Let us drop the id column by running the following command:

ALTER TABLE colleagues DROP id;

```
mysql> ALTER TABLE colleagues DROP id;
Query OK, 4 rows affected (0.40 sec)
Records: 4  Duplicates: 0  Warnings: 0

mysql>
```

To confirm whether the deletion has taken place, let's take a look at the table data:

```
mysql> select * from colleagues;
+-----------+-------------+
| name      | home_city   |
+-----------+-------------+
| John      | New Delhi   |
| Joel      | New Jersey  |
| Britney   | New York    |
| Biggy     | Washington  |
+-----------+-------------+
4 rows in set (0.00 sec)

mysql>
```

The deletion was successful. We combined the ALTER TABLE and the DROP commands for the deletion of the column. Now, let us re-add the column to the table:

ALTER TABLE colleagues

ADD id INT UNSIGNED NOT NULL AUTO_INCREMENT FIRST,

ADD PRIMARY KEY (id);

The command should run as follows:

```
mysql> ALTER TABLE colleagues
    ->     ADD id INT UNSIGNED NOT NULL AUTO_INCREMENT FIRST,
    ->     ADD PRIMARY KEY (id);
Query OK, 0 rows affected (0.76 sec)
Records: 0  Duplicates: 0  Warnings: 0
```

We started with the ALTER TABLE command to specify the name of the table we need to change. The ADD command has then been used to add the column and set it as the primary key for the table. We have also used the auto_increment property in the column definition. We can now query the table to see what has happened:

```
mysql> ALTER TABLE colleagues
    ->     ADD id INT UNSIGNED NOT NULL AUTO_INCREMENT FIRST,
    ->     ADD PRIMARY KEY (id);
Query OK, 0 rows affected (0.76 sec)
Records: 0  Duplicates: 0  Warnings: 0

mysql> select * from colleagues;
+----+---------+------------+
| id | name    | home_city  |
+----+---------+------------+
|  1 | John    | New Delhi  |
|  2 | Joel    | New Jersey |
|  3 | Britney | New York   |
|  4 | Biggy   | Washington |
+----+---------+------------+
4 rows in set (0.00 sec)

mysql>
```

The id column was added successfully. The sequence has also been numbered correctly.

MySQL starts the sequence at index 1 by default. However, it is possible for you to customize this when you are creating the table. You can set the limit or amount of the increment each time a record is created. Like in the table named colleagues, we can alter the table for the auto_increment to be done at intervals of 2. This is achieved through the code below:

ALTER TABLE colleagues AUTO_INCREMENT = 2;

The command should run successfully, as shown below:

```
mysql> ALTER TABLE colleagues AUTO_INCREMENT = 2;
Query OK, 0 rows affected (0.06 sec)
Records: 0  Duplicates: 0  Warnings: 0

mysql>
```

We can specify where the auto_increment will start at the time of the creation of the table. The following example shows this:

CREATE TABLE colleagues2

(

id INT UNSIGNED NOT NULL AUTO_INCREMENT = 10,

PRIMARY KEY (id),

name VARCHAR(20) NOT NULL,

home_city VARCHAR(20) NOT NULL

);

From the above instance, we set the auto_increment property on the id column, and the initial value for the column will be 10.

Chapter 9: 14-SQL Subqueries

A sub-query refers to a query embedded inside another query, and this is done in the *WHERE* clause. It is also referred to as an Inner query or Nested query.

We use a sub-query to return the data that will be used in our main query and as a condition for restricting the data we are to retrieve. We can add sub-queries to *SELECT, UPDATE, INSERT,* and DELETE statements and combine them with operators like =, <, >, <=, >=, *IN, BETWEEN* and many others.

The following are the rules that govern the use of sub-queries:

·	A sub-query must be added within parenthesis.

·	A sub-query should return only one column, meaning that the SELECT * cannot be used within a sub-query unless where the table has only a single column. If your goal is to perform row comparison, you can create a sub-query that will return multiple columns.

·	One can only create sub-queries that return over one row with multiple value operators like IN and NOT IN operators.

· You cannot use a UNION in a sub-query. You are only allowed to use one SELECT statement.

· Your SELECT list should not include a reference to values testing to a BLOB, CLOB, ARRAY, or NCLOB.

· You cannot immediately enclose a sub-query within a set function.

· You cannot use the BETWEEN operator with a sub-query. However, you can use this operator within a sub-query.

Subqueries with SELECT Statement

In most cases, we use subqueries with the SQL's SELECT statement.

We do this using the syntax given below:

SELECT columnName [, columnName]

FROM table_1 [, table_2]

WHERE columnName **OPERATOR**

  (**SELECT** columnName [,columnName]

  FROM table_1 [, table_2]

  [**WHERE**])

Consider the students table with the data given below:

Let us now create a query with a sub-query as shown below:

SELECT *

   FROM students

   WHERE regno **IN** (**SELECT** regno

      FROM students

      WHERE age >= 19);

The command should return the result given below:

We have used the following subquery:

SELECT regno

      FROM students

      WHERE age >= 19;

In the main query, we are using the results of the above subquery to return our final results. This means that the main query will only return the records of students whose age is 19 and above. That is what the above output shows.

Subqueries with INSERT Statement

We can also use Sub-queries with the INSERT statement. What happens, in this case, is that the insert statement will use the data that has been returned by the query to insert it into another table. It is possible for us to change the data that the sub-query returns using date, character or number functions.

The following syntax shows how we can add a sub-query to the INSERT statement:

INSERT INTO tableName [(column_1 [, column_2])]

   SELECT [*|column_1 [, column_2]

   FROM table_1 [, table_2]

   [**WHERE** A **VALUE OPERATOR**]

Consider a situation in which we have the table students2 which is an exact copy of the **students'** table. First, let us create this table:

CREATE TABLE students2 **LIKE** students**;**

The table doesn't have even a single record. We need to populate it with data from the students' table. We then run the following query to perform this task:

INSERT INTO students2

SELECT * **FROM** students

WHERE regno **IN** (**SELECT** regno

FROM students);

The code should run successfully as shown below:

We have used the regno column of the table named **students** to select all the records in that table and populate them into the table named **students2**. Let us query the table to see its contents:

It is clear that the table was populated successfully.

 Subqueries with UPDATE Statement

We can combine the update statement with a sub-query. With this, we can update either single or multiple columns in a table.

We can do this using the following syntax:

UPDATE table

SET columnName = newValue

[**WHERE OPERATOR** [**VALUE**]

  (**SELECT** COLUMNNAME

FROM TABLENAME)

[**WHERE**)]

We need to show using the students' table. The table has the data given below:

The table students2 is a copy of the students' table. We need to increase the ages of the students by 1. This means we run the following command:

UPDATE students

SET age= age + 1

WHERE regno **IN** (**SELECT** regno **FROM** students2);

The command should run successfully as shown below:

```
mysql> UPDATE students
    ->     SET age= age + 1
    ->     WHERE regno IN (SELECT regno FROM students2 );
Query OK, 5 rows affected (0.08 sec)
Rows matched: 5  Changed: 5  Warnings: 0

mysql>
```

Since the two tables have exactly the same data, all the records in the students' table were matched to the sub-query. This means that all the records were updated. To confirm this, we run a select statement against the students' table:

The above figure shows that the values of age were increased by 1.

Subqueries with DELETE Statement

We can use sub-queries with the DELETE statement just like the other SQL statements. The following syntax shows how we can do this:

DELETE FROM TABLENAME

[**WHERE OPERATOR** [**VALUE**]

  (**SELECT** COLUMNNAME

  FROM TABLENAME)

  [**WHERE**)]

Suppose we need to make a deletion on the students table. The students table has the following data:

The **students2** table is an exact copy of the above table as shown below:

We need to perform a deletion on the students table by running the following command:

DELETE FROM students

  WHERE AGE **IN** (**SELECT** age **FROM** students2

    WHERE AGE < 20);

The command should run successfully as shown below:

The record in which the value of age is below 20 will be deleted. This is because this is what the subqueries return. We can confirm this by running a select statement on the students' table as shown below:

The above output shows that the record was deleted successfully.

Chapter 10: Database Components

Now that you know more about a database's use in the real world and why you may want to learn SQL, we will dive into the components of the database.

These components or items within a database are typically referred to as "objects". These objects can range from tables, to columns, to indexes and even triggers. Essentially, these are all of the pieces of the data puzzle that make up the database itself.

The examples and screenshots used in the following sections are from the AdventureWorks2012 database, which you will be working with later on in this book.

Database Tables

Within the database are tables, which hold the data itself. A table consists of columns that are the headers of the table, like First_Name and Last_Name, for example. There are also rows, which are considered an entry within the table. The point to where the column and row intersect is called a cell.

The cell is where the data is shown, like someone's actual first name and last name. Some cells may not always have data, which is considered NULL in the database. This just means that no data exists in that cell.

In Microsoft's SQL Server, a table can have up to 1,024 columns, but can have any number of rows.

Schemas

A schema is considered a logical container for the tables. It's essentially, a way to group tables together based on the type of data that they hold. It won't affect an end user who interacts with the database, like someone who runs reports. But one who works directly with the database, like a database administrator or a developer, will see the available schemas.

Consider a realistic example of several tables containing data for Sales records. There may be several tables named Sales_Order, Sales_History or Sales_Customer. You can put all of these Sales tables into a "Sales" schema to better identify them when you work directly with the database.

Columns

Remember that you can only have up to 1,024 columns in a given table in SQL Server!

Rows and NULL values

A row is considered an entry in a table. The row will be one line across, and typically have data within each column. Though, in some cases, there may be a NULL value in one or many cells.

Back to our example of names, most people have first and last names, but not everyone has a middle name. In that case, a row would have values in the first and last name columns, but not the middle name column, like shown below.

Primary Keys

A primary key is a constraint on a column that forces every value in that column to be unique. By forcing uniqueness on values in that column, it helps maintain the integrity of the data and helps prevent any future data issues.

A realistic example of a primary key would be an employee ID or a sales record ID. You wouldn't want to have two of the same employee ID's for two different people, nor would you want to have two or more of the same sales record ID's for different sales transactions. That would be a nightmare when trying to store and retrieve data!

You can see in the below example that each value for BusinessEntityID is unique for every person.

Foreign Keys

Another key similar to the primary key is a foreign key. These differ from primary keys by not always being unique and act as a link between two or more tables.

Below is an example of a foreign key that exists in the AdventureWorks2012 database. The foreign key is ProductID in this table (Sales.SalesOrderDetail):

The ProductID in the above table is linking to the ProductID (primary key) in the Production.Product table:

Essentially, foreign keys will check its link to the other table to see if that value exists. If not, then you will end up receiving an error when trying to insert data into the table where the foreign key is.

Constraints

Primary keys and foreign keys are known as constraints in the database. Constraints are "rules" that are set in place as far as the types of data that can be entered. There are several others that are used aside from primary keys and foreign keys that help maintain the integrity of the data.

UNIQUE – enforces all values in that column to be different. An example of this could be applied to the Production.Product table. Each product should be different, since you wouldn't want to store the same product name multiple times.

NOT NULL – ensures that no value in that column is NULL. This could also be applied to the same table as above. In this case, the ProductNumber cannot have a NULL value, as each Product should have its own corresponding ProductNumber.

DEFAULT – sets a default value in a column when a value is not provided. A great example of this would be the ListPrice column. When a value isn't specified when being added to this table, the value will default to 0.00. If this value were to be calculated in another table and be a NULL value (like a sales table where sales from the company are made), then it would be impossible to calculate based on a NULL value since it's not a number. Using a default value of 0.00 is a better approach.

INDEXES – Indexes are constraints that are created on a column that speeds up the retrieval of data. An index will essentially compile all of the values in a column and treat them as unique values, even if they're not. By treating them as unique values, it allows the database engine to improve its search based on that column.

Indexes are best used on columns that:

- Do not have a unique constraint
- Are not a primary key
- Or are not a foreign key

The reason for not applying an index to a column that satisfies any of the above three conditions, is that these are naturally faster for retrieving data since they are constraints.

As an example, an index would be best used on something like a date column in a sales table. You may be filtering certain transaction dates from January through March as part of your quarterly reports, yet see many purchases on the same day between those months. By treating it as a unique column, even the same or similar values can still be found much quicker by the database engine.

Views

A view is a virtual table that's comprised of one or more columns from one or more tables. It is created using a SQL query and the original code used to create the view is recompiled when a user queries that table.

In addition, any updates to data made in the originating tables (i.e. the tables and columns that make up the view) will be pulled into the view to show current data. This is another reason that views are great for reporting purposes, as you can pull real-time data without touching the origin tables.

For best practices, DO NOT update any data in a view. If you need to update the data for any reason, perform that in the originating table(s).

To expand a little bit on why a view would be used is the following:

1. To hide the raw elements of the database from the end-user so that they only see what they need to. You can also make it more cryptic for the end-user.

2. An alternative to queries that are frequently run in the database, like reporting purposes as an example.

These are only a few reasons as to why you would use a view. However, depending on your situation, there could be other reasons why you would use a view instead of writing a query to directly obtain data from one or more tables.

To better illustrate the concept of a view, the below example has two tables: 'People' and 'Locations'. These two tables are combined into a view that is called 'People and Locations' just for simplicity. These are also joined on a common field, i.e. the LocationID.

Stored Procedures

Stored procedures are pre-compiled SQL syntax that can be used over and over again by executing its name in SQL Server. If there's a certain query that you're running frequently and writing it from scratch or saving the file somewhere and then opening it to be able to run it, then it may be time to consider creating a stored procedure out of that query.

Just like with SQL syntax that you'd write from scratch and passing in a value for your WHERE clause, you can do the same with a stored procedure. You have the ability to pass in certain values to achieve the end result that you're looking for. Though, you don't always have to pass a parameter into a stored procedure.

As an example, let's say that as part of the HR department, you must run a query once a month to verify which employees are salary and non-salary, in compliance with labor laws and company policy.

Instead of opening a file frequently or writing the code from scratch, you can simply call the stored procedure that you saved in the database, to retrieve the information for you. You would just specify the proper value (where 1 is TRUE and 0 is FALSE in this case).

EXEC　　　　　**HumanResources.SalariedEmployees @SalariedFlag = 1**

In the result set below, you can see some of the employees who work in a salary type position:

Triggers

A trigger in the database is a stored procedure (pre-compiled code) that will execute when a certain event happens to a table. Generally, these triggers will fire off when data is added, updated or deleted from a table.

Below is an example of a trigger that prints a message when a new department is created in the HumanResources.Department table.

--Creates a notification stating that a new department has been created

--when an INSERT statement is executed against the Department table

CREATE TRIGGER NewDepartment

ON HumanResources.Department

AFTER INSERT

    AS RAISERROR ('A new department has been created.', *10*, *9*)

To expand on this a little more, you specify the name of your trigger after CREATE TRIGGER. After ON, you'll specify the table name that this is associated with.

Next, you can specify which type of action will fire this trigger (you may also use UPDATE and/or DELETE), which is known as a DML trigger in this case.

Last, I'm printing a message that a new department has been created and using some number codes in SQL Server for configuration.

To see this trigger in the works, here's the INSERT statement I'm using to create a new department. There are four columns in this table, DepartmentID, Name, GroupName and ModifiedDate. I'm skipping the DepartmentID column in the INSERT statement because a new ID is automatically generated by the database engine.

  --Adding a new department to the Department's table

    INSERT INTO HumanResources.Department

(**Name**, GroupName, ModifiedDate)

VALUES

**('Business Analysis', 'Research and Development',
GETDATE()) --GETDATE() gets the current date
and time, depending on the data type being used
in the table**

The trigger will prompt a message after the new record
has been successfully inserted.

A new department has been created.

(1 row(s) affected)

If I were to run a query against this table, I can see that
my department was successfully added as well.

Deadlocks in SQL

 In most of the cases, multiple users access database
applications simultaneously, which means that multiple
transactions are being executed on database in parallel.

By default when a transaction performs an operation on a database resource such as a table, it locks the resource. During that period, no other transaction can access the locked resource. Deadlocks occur when two or more than two processes try to access resources that are locked by the other processes participating in the deadlock.

Deadlocks are best explained with the help of an example. Consider a scenario where some transactionA has performed an operation on tableA and has acquired lock on the table. Similarly, there is another transaction named transactionB that is executing in parallel and performs some operation on tableB. Now, transactionA wants to perform some operation on tableBwhich is already locked by transactionB. Similarly, transactionB wants to perform an operation on tableA, but it is already locked by transactionA. This results in a deadlock since transactionA is waiting on a resource locked by transactionB, which is waiting on a resource locked by transactionA. In this chapter we shall see a practical example of deadlocks. Then we will see how we can analyze and resolve deadlocks.

Dummy Data Creation

For the sake of this chapter, we will create a dummy database. This database will be used in the deadlock example that we shall in next section. Execute the following script

```
CREATE DATABASE dldb;

GO
  USE dldb;

  CREATE TABLE tableA

(

  id INT IDENTITY PRIMARY KEY,

  patient_name NVARCHAR(50)

)

  INSERT INTO tableA VALUES ('Thomas')

  CREATE TABLE tableB

(

  id INT IDENTITY PRIMARY KEY,

  patient_name NVARCHAR(50)

)

  INSERT INTO table2 VALUES ('Helene')
```

The above script creates database named "dldb". In the database we create two tables: tableA and tableB. We then insert one record each in the both tables.

Practical Example of Deadlock

Let's write a script that creates deadlock. Open two instances of SQL server management studio. To simulate simultaneous data access, we will run our queries in parallel in these two instances.

 Now, open the first instances of SSMS, and write the following script. Do not execute this script at the moment.

Instance1 Script

USE dldb;

   BEGIN TRANSACTION transactionA

   -- First update statement

   UPDATE tableA SET patient name = 'Thomas - TransactionA'

   WHERE id = 1

   -- Go to the second instance and execute

   -- first update statement

UPDATE tableB SET patient name = 'Helene - TransactionA'

WHERE id = 1

-- Go to the second instance and execute

-- second update statement

COMMIT TRANSACTION

In the second instance, copy and paste the following script. Again, do not run the Script.

Instance 2 Script

USE dldb;

BEGIN TRANSACTION transactionB

-- First update statement

UPDATE tableB SET patient name = 'Helene - TransactionB'

WHERE id = 1

-- Go to the first instance and execute

-- second update statement

UPDATE tableA SET patient name = 'Thomas - TransactionB'

WHERE id = 1

COMMIT TRANSACTION

181

Now we have our scripts ready in both the transaction.

Open both the instances of SSMS side by side as shown in the following figure:

To create a deadlock we have to follow step by step approach. Go to the first instance of SQL Server management studio(SSMS) and execute the following lines from the script:

USE dldb;

BEGIN TRANSACTION transactionA

-- First update statement

UPDATE tableA SET patient name = 'Thomas - TransactionA'

WHERE id = 1

In the above script, transactionA updates the tableAby setting the name of the patient with id one to'Thomas – TransactionA'. At this point of time, transactionA acquires lock on tableA.

Now, execute the following script from the second instance of SSMS.

USE dldb;

BEGIN TRANSACTION transactionB

-- First update statement

UPDATE tableB SET patient name = 'Helene - TransactionB'

WHERE id = 1

The above script executes transactionB which updates tableB by setting the name of patient with id one to'*Helene – TransactionB'*, acquiring lock on tableB.

Now come back again to first instance of SSMS. Execute the following piece of script:

UPDATE tableB SET patient name = 'Helene - TransactionA'

WHERE id = 1

Here transactionA tries to update tableB which is locked by transactionB. Hence transactionA goes to waiting state.

Go to the second instance of SSMS again and execute the following piece of script.

UPDATE tableA SET patient name = 'Thomas - TransactionB'

WHERE id = 1

In the above script, transactionB tries to update tableA which is locked by transactionA. Hence transactionA also goes to waiting state.

At this point of time, transactionA is waiting for a resource locked by transactionB. Similarly, transactionB is waiting for the resource locked by TransactionA. Hence deadlock occurs here.

By default, SSMS selects one of the transactions involved in the deadlock as deadlock victim. The transaction selected as deadlock victim is rolled back, allowing the other transaction to complete its execution. You will see that after few second, the transaction in one of the instances will complete its execution while an error will appear in other instance.

In the example that we just saw, transactionA was allowed to complete its execution while transactionB was selected as deadlock victim. Your result can be different. This is shown in the following figure:

You can see the message "1 row affected" in the instance on the left that is running transactionA. On the other hand in the left instance an error is displayed that reads:

Msg 1205, Level 13, State 51, Line 12
Transaction (Process ID 54) was deadlocked on lock

resources with another process and has been chosen

as the deadlock victim. Rerun the transaction.

The error says that the Transaction with process ID 54 was involved in a deadlock and hence chosen as victim of the deadlock.

Deadlock Analysis and Prevention

In the previous section we generated deadlock ourselves, therefore we have information about the processes involved in the deadlock. In the real world scenarios, this is not the case. Multiple users access the database simultaneously, which often results in deadlocks. However, in such cases we cannot tell which transactions and resources are involved in the deadlock. We need a mechanism that allows us to analyze deadlocks in detail so that we can see what transactions and resources are involved and decide how to resolve the deadlocks. One such ways is via SQL Server error logs.

Reading Deadlock info via SQL Server Error Log

The SQL Server provides only little info about the deadlock. You can get detailed information about the deadlock via SQL error log. However to log deadlock information to error log, first you have to use a trace flag 1222. You can turn trace flag 1222 on global as well as session level. To turn on trace flag 1222 on, execute the following script:

DBCC Traceon(1222, -1)

The above script turns trace flag on global level. If you do not pass the second argument, the trace flag is turned on session level. To see if trace flag is actually turned on, execute the following query:

DBCC TraceStatus(1222)

The above statement results in the following output:

Trace Flag	Status	Global	Session
1222	1	1	0

Here status value 1 shows that trace flag 1222 is on. The 1 for Global column implies that trace flag has been turned on globally.

Now, try to generate a deadlock by following the steps that we performed in the last section. The detailed deadlock information will be logged in the error log. To view sql server error log, you need to execute the following stored procedure.

executesp_readerrorlog

The above stored procedure will retrieve detailed error log a snippet of which is shown below:

Your error log might be different depending upon the databases in your database. The information about all the deadlocks in your database starts with log text "deadlock-list". You may need to scroll down a bit to find this row.

Let's now analyze the log information that is retrieved by the deadlock that we just created. Note that your values will be different for each column, but the information remains same.

ProcessInfo	Text
spid13s	deadlock-list
spid13s	deadlock victim=process1fcf9514ca8
spid13s	process-list
spid13s	process id=process1fcf9514ca8taskpriority=0 logused=308 waitresource=KEY: 8:72057594043105280 (8194443284a0) waittime=921

	ownerId=388813 transactionname=transactionBlasttrans tarted=2017-11-01T15:51:46.547 XDES=0x1fcf8454490 lockMode=X schedulerid=3 kpid=1968 status=suspended spid=57 sbid=0 ecid=0 priority=0 trancount=2 lastbatchstarted=2017-11-01T15:51:54.380 lastbatchcompleted=2017-11-01T15:51:54.377 lastattention=1900-01-01T00:00:00.377 clientapp=Microsoft SQL Server Management Studio - Query hostname=DESKTOP-GLQ5VRA hostpid=968 loginname=DESKTOP-GLQ5VRA\Mani isolationlevel=read committed (2) xactid=388813 currentdb=8 lockTimeout=4294967295 clientoption1=671090784 clientoption2=390200
spid13s	executionStack
spid13s	frame procname=adhoc line=2 stmtstart=58 stmtend=164 sqlhandle=0x0200000014b61731ad79b 1eec6740c98aab3ab91bd31af4d00000 00000000000000000000000000000000 0000
spid13s	unknown

spid13s	frame procname=adhoc line=2 stmtstart=4 stmtend=142 sqlhandle=0x0200000080129b021f706 41be5a5e43a1ca1ef67e9721c9700000 00000000000000000000000000000000 0000
spid13s	unknown
spid13s	inputbuf
spid13s	UPDATE tableA SET patient_name = 'Thomas - TransactionB'
spid13s	WHERE id = 1
spid13s	process id=process1fcf9515468taskpriority=0 logused=308 waitresource=KEY: 8:72057594043170816 (8194443284a0) waittime=4588 ownerId=388767 transactionname=transactionAlasttrans tarted=2017-11-01T15:51:44.383 XDES=0x1fcf8428490 lockMode=X schedulerid=3 kpid=11000 status=suspended spid=54 sbid=0 ecid=0 priority=0 trancount=2 lastbatchstarted=2017-11-01T15:51:50.710 lastbatchcompleted=2017-11-01T15:51:50.710 lastattention=1900-01-01T00:00:00.710 clientapp=Microsoft SQL Server Management Studio - Query

	hostname=DESKTOP-GLQ5VRA hostpid=1140 loginname=DESKTOP-GLQ5VRA\Mani isolationlevel=read committed (2) xactid=388767 currentdb=8 lockTimeout=4294967295 clientoption1=671090784 clientoption2=390200
spid13s	executionStack
spid13s	frame procname=adhoc line=1 stmtstart=58 stmtend=164 sqlhandle=0x02000000ec86cd1dbe1cd 7fc97237a12abb461f1fc27e278000000 0000000000000000000000000000000 000
spid13s	unknown
spid13s	frame procname=adhoc line=1 stmtend=138 sqlhandle=0x020000003a45a10eb863d 6370a5f99368760983cacbf4895000000 0000000000000000000000000000000 000
spid13s	unknown
spid13s	inputbuf
spid13s	UPDATE tableB SET patient_name = 'Helene - TransactionA'
spid13s	WHERE id = 1
spid13s	resource-list

spid13s	keylockhobtid=720575940043105280 dbid=8 *objectname=dldb.dbo.tableA*indexname =PK__tableA__3213E83F1C2C4D64 id=lock1fd004bd600　　　　mode=X associatedObjectId=720575940431052 80
spid13s	owner-list
spid13s	owner　　id=process1fcf9515468 mode=X
spid13s	waiter-list
spid13s	waiter　　id=process1fcf9514ca8 mode=X requestType=wait
spid13s	keylockhobtid=720575940043170816 dbid=8 *objectname=dldb.dbo.tableB*indexname =PK__tableB__3213E83FFE08D6AB id=lock1fd004c2200　　　　mode=X associatedObjectId=720575940431708 16
spid13s	owner-list
spid13s	owner　　id=process1fcf9514ca8 mode=X
spid13s	waiter-list
spid13s	waiter　　id=process1fcf9515468 mode=X requestType=wait

The deadlock information logged by the SQL server error log has three main parts.

1-___The deadlock Victim

2-___Process List

The process list is the list of all the processes involved in a deadlock. In the deadlock that we generated, two processes were involved. In the processes list you can see details of both of these processes. The id of the first process is highlighted in red whereas the id of the second process is highlighted in green. Notice that in the process list, the first process is the process that has been selected as deadlock victim too.

Apart from process id, there you can also see other information about the processes. For instance, you can find login information of the process, the isolation level of the process etc. You can see the script that the process was trying to run. For instance if you look at the first process in the process list, you can find that it was trying to update the patient_name column of the table tableA, when the deadlock occurred.

3-___Resource List

The resource list contains information about the resources that were involved in the deadlock. In our example, tableA and tableB were the only two resources involved in the deadlock. You can both of these tables highlighted in blue in the resource list of the log in the table above.

Some tips for Deadlock Avoidance

From the error log we can get detailed information about the deadlock. However we can minimize the chance of deadlock occurrence if we follow these tips:

- *Execute transactions in a single batch and keep them short*
- *Release resources automatically after a certain time period*
- *Sequential resource sharing*
- Not allowing user to interact with the application when transactions are being executed.

This chapter presented a brief overview to deadlocks. In the next chapter, we shall see another extremely useful concept, i.e. Cursors.

Chapter 11: How to Manage Database Objects

This chapter will discuss database objects: their nature, behaviors, storage requirements, and interrelatedness. Basically, databases objects are the backbone of relational databases. You use these objects to store data (i.e. they are logical units found inside a database). For this reason, these objects are also called back-end databases.

What is a Database Object?

Database objects are the defined objects within a database utilized to save or retrieve information. Here are several examples of database objects: views, clusters, tables, indexes, synonyms, and sequences.

The Schema

A schema is a set of database objects linked to a certain database user. This user, known as the "schema owner," owns the set of objects linked to his/her username. Simply put, any person who generates an object has just generated his/her own schema. That means users have control over database objects that are generated, deleted, and manipulated.

Let's assume that you received login credentials (i.e. username and password) from a database administrator. The username is PERSON1. Let's say you accessed the database and created a table named EMPLOYEES_TBL. In the database's records, the file's actual name is PERSON1.EMPLOYEES_TBL. The table's "schema name" is PERSON1, which is also the creator/owner of that table.

When accessing a schema that you own, you are not required to use the schema name. That means you have two ways of accessing the imaginary file given above. These are:

- PERSON1.EMPLOYEES_TBL

- EMPLOYEES_TBL

As you can see, the second option involves fewer characters. This is the reason why schema owners prefer this method of accessing their files. If other users want to view the file, however, they must include the schema in their database query.

The screenshot below shows two schemas within a database.

Tables – The Main Tool for Storing Data

Modern database users consider tables as the main storage tool. In general, a table is formed by row/s and column/s. Tables take up space within a database and may be temporary or permanent.

Fields/Columns

Fields, referred to as columns when working with a relational database, are parts of a table where a particular data type is assigned to. You should name a field so that it matches the data type it will be used with. You may specify fields as NULL (i.e. nothing should be entered) or NOT NULL (i.e. something needs to be entered).

Each table should have at least one field. Fields are the elements inside a table that store certain kinds of data (e.g. names, addresses, phone numbers, etc.). For instance, you'll find a "customer name" column when checking a database table for customer information.

Rows

Rows are records of data within a table. For instance, a row in a customer database table might hold the name, fax number, and identification number of a certain customer. Rows are composed of fields that hold information from a single record in the table.

SQL Statement – CREATE TABLE

"CREATE TABLE" is an SQL statement used to generate a table. Even though you can create tables quickly and easily, you should spend time and effort in planning the structures of your new table. That means you have to do some research and planning before issuing this SQL statement.

Here are some of the questions you should answer when creating tables:

- What kind of data am I working on?
- What name should I choose for this table?
- What column will form the main key?
- What names should be assigned to the fields/columns?
- What type of data can be assigned to those columns?
- Which columns can be empty?

- What is the maximum length for every column?

Once you have answered these questions, using the CREATE TABLE command becomes simple.

Here's the syntax to generate a new table:

The final character of that statement is a semicolon. Almost all SQL implementations use certain characters to terminate statements or submit statements to the server. MySQL and Oracle use semicolons to perform these functions. Transact-SQL, on the other hand, utilizes the "GO" command. To make this book consistent, statements will be terminated or submitted using a semicolon.

The STORAGE Clause

Some SQL implementations offer STORAGE clauses. These clauses help you in assigning the table sizes. That means you can use them while creating tables. MySQL uses the following syntax for its STORAGE clause:

The Naming Conventions

When naming database objects, particularly columns and tables, you should choose names that reflect the data they will be used for. For instance, you may use the name EMPLOYEES_TBL for a table used to hold employee information. You need to name columns using the same principle. A column used to store the phone number of employees may be named PHONE_NUMBER.

SQL Command - ALTER TABLE

You can use ALTER TABLE, a powerful SQL command, to modify existing database tables. You may add fields, remove columns, change field definitions, include or exclude constraints, and, in certain SQL implementations, change the table's STORAGE values. Here's the syntax for this command:

Altering the Elements of a Database Table

A column's "attributes" refer to the laws and behaviors of data inside that column. You may change a column's attributes using ALTER TABLE. Here, the term "attributes" refers to:

- The type of data assigned to a column.
- The scale, length, or precision of a column.
- Whether you can enter NULL values into a column.

In the screenshot below, ALTER TABLE is used on the EMPLOYEE_TBL to change the attributes of a column named EMP_ID:

If you are using MySQL, you'll get the following statement:

Adding Columns to a Database Table

You must remember certain rules when adding columns to existing database tables. One of the rules is this: You can't add a NOT NULL column if the table has data in it. Basically, you should use NOT NULL to indicate that the column should hold some value for each data row within the table. If you'll add a NOT NULL column, you will go against this new constraint if the current data rows don't have specific values for the added column.

Modifying Fields/Columns

Here are the rules you should follow when altering existing columns:

- You can always increase a column's length.
- You can decrease a column's length only if the highest value for the column is lower than or equal to the desired length.
- You can always increase the quantity of digits for numeric data types.
- You can only decrease the quantity of digits for numeric data types if the value of the largest

quantity of digits in the column is lower than or equal to the desired quantity of digits.

- You can increase or decrease the quantity of decimal places for numeric data types.
- You can easily change the data type of any column.

Important Note: Be extremely careful when changing or dropping tables. You might lose valuable information if you will commit typing or logical mistakes while executing these SQL statements.

How to Create New Tables from Existing Ones

You may duplicate an existing table using these SQL statements: (1) CREATE TABLE and (2) SELECT. After executing these statements, you'll get a new table whose column definitions are identical to that of the old one. This feature is customizable: you may copy all of the columns or just the ones you need. The columns generated using this pair of statements will assume the size needed to store the information. Here's the main syntax for generating a table from an existing one:

This syntax involves a new keyword (i.e. SELECT). This keyword can help you perform database queries. In modern database systems, SELECT can help you generate tables using search results.

How to Drop Tables

You can drop tables easily. If you used the RESTRICT statement and referenced the table using a view/constraint, the DROP command will give you an error message. If you used CASCASE, however, DROP will succeed and all constraints and/or views will be dropped. The syntax for dropping a table is:

Important Note: When dropping a database table, specify the owner or schema name of the table you are working on. This is important since dropping the wrong table can result to loss of data. If you can access multiple database accounts, make sure that you are logged in to the right account prior to dropping any table.

The Integrity Constraints

You can use integrity constraints to ensure the consistency and accuracy of data within a database. In general, database users handle integrity concerns through a concept called "Referential Integrity." In this section, you'll learn about the integrity constraints that you can use in SQL.

Primary Key

A primary key is used to determine columns that make data rows unique. You can form primary keys using one or more columns. For instance, either the product's name or an assigned reference number can serve as a primary key for a product table. The goal is to provide each record with a unique detail or primary key. In general, you can assign a primary key during table creation.

In the example below, the table's primary key is the column named EMP_ID.

You can assign primary keys this way while creating a new table. In this example, the table's primary key is an implicit condition. As an alternative, you may specify primary keys as explicit conditions while creating a table. Here's an example:

In the example given above, the primary key is given after the comma list.

If you need to form a primary key using multiple columns, you use this method:

Unique Column Constraint

Unique column constraints are similar to primary keys: the column should have a unique value for each row. While you need to place a primary key in a single column, you may place unique constraints on different columns. Here's an example:

In the example above, EMP_ID serves as the primary key. That means the column for employee identification numbers is being used to guarantee the uniqueness of each record. Users often reference primary key columns for database queries, especially when merging tables. The EMP_PHONE column has a unique value, which means each employee has a unique phone number.

Foreign Key

You can use this key while working on parent and child tables. Foreign keys are columns in a child table that points to a primary key inside the parent table. This type of key serves as the primary tool in enforcing referential integrity within a database. You may use a foreign key column to reference a primary key from a different table.

In the example below, you'll learn how to create a foreign key:

Here, EMP_ID serves as a foreign key for a table named EMPLOYEE_PAY_TBL. This key points to the EMP_ID section of another table (i.e. the EMPLOYEE_TBL table). With this key, the database administrator can make sure that each EMP_ID inside the EMPLOYEE_PAY_TBL has a corresponding entry in EMPLOYEE_TBL. SQL practitioners call this the "parent/child relationship."

Study the following figure. This will help you to understand the relationship between child tables and parent tables.

How to Drop Constraints

You can use the option "DROP CONSTAINT" to drop the constraints (e.g. primary key, foreign key, unique column, etc.) you applied for your tables. For instance, if you want to remove the primary key in a table named "EMPLOYEES", you may use this command:

Some SQL implementations offer shortcuts for removing constraints. Oracle, for instance, uses this command to drop a primary key constraint:

On the other hand, certain SQL implementations allow users to deactivate constraints. Rather than dropping constraints permanently, you may disable them temporarily. This way, you can reactivate the constraints you will need in the future.

Chapter 12: Database Advance Topics

In this chapter you will be introduced to some advance topics in SQL that goes beyond basic database transactions. Even if this section only includes an overview of cursors, triggers and errors, such knowledge could possibly help you extend the features of your SQL implementations.

Cursors

Generally, SQL commands manipulate database objects using set-based operations. This means that transactions are performed on a group or block of data. A cursor, on the other hand, processes data from a table one row at a time. It is created using a compound a statement and destroyed upon exit. The standard syntax for declaring a cursor is (which may differ for every implementation):

DECLARE CURSOR CURSOR_NAME
IS {SELECT_STATEMENT}

You can perform operations on a cursor only after it has been declared or defined.

- Open a Cursor

Once declared, you perform an OPEN operation to access the cursor and then execute the specified SELECT statement. The results of the SELECT query will be saved in a certain area in the memory. The standard syntax for opening a cursor is:

OPEN **CURSOR_NAME**;

- Fetch Data from a Cursor

The FETCH statement is performed if you want to retrieve the query results or the data from the cursor. The standard syntax for fetching data is:

FETCH   NEXT   FROM   **CURSOR_NAME**   [INTO **FETCH_LIST**]

In SQL programming, the optional statement inside the square brackets will let you assign the data retrieved into a certain variable.

- Close a Cursor

There is a corresponding CLOSE statement to be executed when you open a particular cursor. Once the cursor is closed, all the names and resources used will be deallocated. Thus, the cursor is no longer available for the program to use. The standard syntax for closing a cursor is:

CLOSE **CURSOR_NAME**

Triggers

There are instances when you want certain SQL operations or transactions to occur after performing some specific actions. This scenario describes an SQL statement that triggers another SQL statement to take place. Essentially, a trigger is an SQL procedure that is compiled in the database that execute certain transactions based on other transactions that have previously occurred. Such triggers can be performed before or after the execution of DML statements (INSERT, DELETE and UPDATE). In addition, triggers can validate data integrity, maintain data consistency, undo transactions, log operations, modify and read data values in different databases.

- Create a Trigger

The standard syntax for creating a trigger is:

CREATE TRIGGER ***TRIGGER_NAME***

   TRIGGER_ACTION_TIMETRIGGER_E

VENT

ON TABLE_NAME

[REFERENCING

OLD_OR_NEW_VALUE_ALIAS_LIST**]**

TRIGGERED_ACTION

TRIGGER_NAME - the unique identifying name for this object

TRIGGER_ACTION_TIMETRIGGER_EVENT - the specified time that the set of triggered actions will occur (whether before or after the triggering event).

TABLE_NAME – the table for which the DML statements have been specified

TRIGGERED_ACTION – specifies the actions to be performed once an event is triggered

Once a trigger has been created, it cannot be altered anymore. You can just either re-create or replace it. How a trigger works depends what conditions you specify – whether it will fire at once when a DML statement is performed or it will fire multiple times for every table row affected by the DML statement. You can also include a threshold value or a Boolean condition, that when such condition is met will trigger a course of action.

- Drop a Trigger

The basic syntax for dropping a trigger is the same as dropping a table or a view:

DROP TRIGGER TRIGGER_NAME;

Errors

An error-free design or implementation is one of the ultimate goals in any programming language. You can commit errors by simply not following naming conventions, improperly writing the programming codes (syntax or typo errors like a missing apostrophe or parenthesis) or even when the data entered does not match the data type defined.

To make things easier, SQL has devised a way to return error information so that programmers will be aware of what is going on and be able to undertake the appropriate actions to correct the situation. Some of these error-handling mechanisms are the status parameter SQLSTATE and the WHENEVER clause.

- SQLSTATE

The status parameter or host variable SQLSTATE is an error-handling tool that includes a wide selection of anomalous condition. It is a string that consists of five characters (uppercase letters from A to Z and numerals from 0 to 9), where the first two characters refer to the class code while the next three is the subclass code. The class code identifies the status after an SQL statement has been completed – whether it is successful or not (if not successful, then one of the major types of error conditions are returned). Supplementary information about the execution of the SQL statement is also indicated in the subclass code.

The SQLSTATE is updated after every operation. If the value is '00000' (five zeroes), it means that the execution was successful and you can proceed to the next operation. If it contains a five-character string other than '00000', then you have to check your programming lines to rectify the error committed. There are numerous ways on how to handle a certain SQL error, depending on the class code and subclass code specified in the SQLSTATE.

- WHENEVER Clause

The WHENEVER clause error-handling mechanism focuses on execution exceptions. With this, an error is acknowledged and gives the programmer the option to correct it. This is better than not being able to do something if an error occurs. If you cannot rectify or reverse the error that was committed, then you can just gracefully terminate the application program.

*WHENEVER **CONDITION ACTION**;*

CONDITION – value can either be SQLERROR (returns TRUE if SQLSTATE class code is other than 00, 01 or 02) or NOT FOUND (returns TRUE if SQLSTATE is 02000)

ACTION – value can either be CONTINUE (execution of the program is continued normally) or GOTO address (execution of a designated program address)

In this chapter you have learnt the primary role of cursors, how triggers work and the importance of handling errors in SQL programming. Learning these advance topics is one step closer in maximizing the potentials of your SQL implementations.

Chapter 13: Clauses and Queries

In this chapter we'll be dealing with clauses and queries. A query, is, simply put, a set of instructions you give in order to change a table within a database. The ones we will be looking at in this chapter are primarily the UPDATE and DELETE queries.

While you should have learned about other queries prior to reading this book, these two are the building blocks of any SQL developer worth their salt.

Both of these queries are very self-explanatory. The UPDATE query will take the information currently within a table, and change it to whatever you desire. The DELETE query is quite like an UPDATE query just with "null" instead of what you wanted to change it to. It will delete any entries that you wish.

It is important to note that while these queries are extremely important, they're also inefficient. You'll learn later on that there are much more efficient ways to do what these queries do, and at a much larger scale.

With that being said, they are still a must-learn for budding developers. They help you learn the fundamental blocks that advanced SQL is based on.

After all, every business owner has heard horror stories of developers that only know higher-level material, and low-level techniques become their downfall.

These queries will primarily be useful in debugging and lower-level positions. Otherwise, they're only useful for manually editing smaller tables, at which point you might as well use Excel instead of SQL.

On the other side of the coin, we have the TOP query. The TOP query, rather than actually changing the information inside a table, shows you only specific entries from a table. To be precise, the TOP query will show you the topmost N or topmost N % of a given table.

This is especially useful if you're using SQL for maths or science, in which case it can make recurring certain functions very easy.

Besides that, this chapter will also cover the LIKE and ORDER BY clauses. The LIKE clause is meant to compare different objects/strings while the ORDER BY clause will sort a table in ascending or descending order, as you feel fit.

These are two extremely powerful tools that you'll use throughout your career as a SQL developer, so let's dive right in!

UPDATE & DELETE Query

The UPDATE query in SQL is mainly intended to be used when modifying the records that are already in a table. What's worth noting here is that if you use the WHERE clause together with the UPDATE query, only the rows you selected with the WHERE clause will be updated. If you don't do this, then every row inside the table will be equally affected.

The Syntax for an UPDATE query within a WHERE clause is:

UPDATE name_of_table

SET column01 = value01, column02=value02..., columnN = valueN

WHERE[your_condition];

When using the UPDATE query, you'll be able to combine any N number of conditions by using the two operators you should be familiar with already: the AND and OR operators.

Take this for example:

In the following table, there are customer records listed, and you're trying to update the record.

You can combine N number of conditions using the AND or the OR operators.

```
+--+----------+-----+-----------+----------+
| ID | NAME     | AGE | ADDRESS   | SALARY  |
+--+----------+-----+-----------+----------+
| 1 | Ilija     | 19 | Uruguay   | 1500.00 |
| 2 | Frank     | 52 | France    | 200.00  |
| 3 | Jim       | 53 | Serbia    | 8040.00 |
| 4 | Martinia| 54 | Amsterdam| 9410.00 |
| 5 | Jaffar    | 66 | Podgorica | 55200.00 |
| 6 | Tim       | 33 | Prune     | 1200.00 |
| 7 | Kit       | 24 | England   | 700.00  |
+--+----------+-----+-----------+----------+
```

Let's say you want to update the address of the customer with the ID number 2, you would do it as such:

SQL> UPDATE CUSTOMER

SET ADDRESS = 'Tom_St'

WHERE ID = 2;

Now, the CUSTOMERS table would have the following records —

```
+--+----------+-----+----------+----------+
| ID | NAME     | AGE | ADDRESS  | SALARY   |
+--+----------+-----+----------+----------+
| 1 | Ilija    | 19 | Uruguay   | 1500.00 |
| 2 | Frank    | 52 | Tom_St    | 200.00 |
| 3 | Jim      | 53 | Serbia    | 8040.00 |
| 4 | Martinia| 54 | Amsterdam| 9410.00 |
| 5 | Jaffar   | 66 | Podgorica | 55200.00 |
| 6 | Tim      | 33 | Prune     | 1200.00 |
| 7 | Kit      | 24 | England   | 700.00 |
+--+----------+-----+----------+----------+
```

Now, if instead, let's say you want to change the salaries and addresses of all your customers, then you won't need to use the WHERE clause. The UPDATE query will handle it all by itself. This can sometimes save quite a bit of time, let's look at the following example:

SQL> UPDATE CUSTOMER

SET ADDRESS = 'Tom_St', SALARY = 1000.00;

Now, CUSTOMERS table would have the following records –

```
+--+----------+-----+-----------+----------+
| ID | NAME     | AGE | ADDRESS   | SALARY   |
+--+----------+-----+-----------+----------+
|  1 | Ilija    |  19 | Tom_St    | 1000.00 |
|  2 | Frank    |  52 | Tom_St    | 1000.00 |
|  3 | Jim      |  53 | Tom_St    | 1000.00 |
|  4 | Martinia|  54 | Tom_St    | 1000.00 |
|  5 | Jaffar   |  66 | Tom_St    | 1000.00 |
|  6 | Tim      |  33 | Tom_St    | 1000.00 |
|  7 | Kit      |  24 | Tom_st    | 1000.00 |
+--+----------+-----+-----------+----------+
```

If you can't really tell where this would be useful, don't worry. There are countless examples from around the corporate world. This will let you replace any given thing in a matter of minutes. While it might not seem practical in a table with 7 people in it, imagine you're Microsoft and instead of 4 columns and 7 rows, you have 50 columns and 7000 rows, that isn't very practical to do by hand now is it?

Now let's take a look at the DELETE query. You can probably imagine what it does. It helps you delete certain records from a table. Now, obviously you don't want your whole table gone, so you should probably use the WHERE clause together with it, so you don't accidentally end up deleting, well, everything. When you use the WHERE clause with the DELETE query, only what you've selected will be deleted. Kind of like clicking on a file and pressing delete on your keyboard.

Let's turn our eyes to the syntax a bit, let's use the customers example again for it.

DELETE FROM name_of_table

WHERE [your_condition];

Similarly to the UPDATE query, you can use this in conjunction with the OR and AND operators to get more complex and precise results. Let's look at the past example we used:

```
+--+----------+-----+-----------+----------+
| ID | NAME | AGE | ADDRESS  | SALARY  |
+--+----------+-----+-----------+----------+
| 1 | Ilija      | 19 | Tom_St   | 1000.00 |
| 2 | Frank    | 52 | Tom_St      | 1000.00 |
```

| 3 | Jim | 53 | Tom_St | 1000.00 |

| 4 | Martinia| 54 | Tom_St | 1000.00 |

| 5 | Jaffar | 66 | Tom_St | 1000.00 |

| 6 | Tim | 33 | Tom_St | 1000.00 |

| 7 | Kit | 24 | Tom_st | 1000.00 |

+--+----------+-----+-----------+----------+

Let's say you want to erase a customer. Maybe they stopped shopping at your locale? Moved to a different state? Whatever reason it may be, this is how you could do it, let's say the customer's number is 7.

SQL> DELETE FROM CUSTOMER

WHERE ID = 7;

As you can see, this is quite similar to the UPDATE query, and they really are similar. If you need some help in thinking about the DELETE query, think about it as an UPDATE query that updates with empty spaces (this isn't entirely accurate, but it helps).

Now the customers table would look like this:

+--+----------+-----+-----------+----------+

| ID | NAME | AGE | ADDRESS | SALARY |

```
+--+----------+-----+----------+---------+
| 1 | Ilija      | 19 | Tom_St   | 1000.00 |
| 2 | Frank      | 52 | Tom_St   | 1000.00 |
| 3 | Jim        | 53 | Tom_St   | 1000.00 |
| 4 | Martinia| 54 | Tom_St | 1000.00 |
| 5 | Jaffar     | 66 | Tom_St   | 1000.00 |
| 6 | Tim        | 33 | Tom_St   | 1000.00 |
+--+----------+-----+----------+---------+
```

As you can see, all that changed is the 7th column is now empty. If you've been wondering how it would look if you hadn't used the WHERE operator, this is how:

```
+--+----------+-----+----------+---------+
+--+----------+-----+----------+---------+
```

That's right! Using the DELETE query without a WHERE operator results in an empty table.

Now, hopefully you won't be using the DELETE query too much wherever you end up working, but it can be useful for a variety of things. For example, when your company is moving servers, or simply purging outdated entries.

Like & Order by Clause

The LIKE clause is utilized when you want to compare two different values. This is done using wildcard operators such as the percent sign and the underscore. Now, while these are the only wildcard operators which are used with the LIKE clause, you'll encounter many more throughout this book.

First, the percentage symbol (%) serves to represent 0, 1 or N characters. Meanwhile the underscore (_) is used to represent only a single digit or symbol. You can also choose to combine these two when it suits you.

The syntax for using the percentage and underscore signs is:

1. - SELECT FROM name_of_table

   WHERE column LIKE '%NNNN%'

2. - SELECT FROM name_of_table

   WHERE column LIKE 'NNNN%'

3. - SELECT FROM name_of_table

   WHERE column LIKE 'NNNN_'

4. - SELECT FROM name_of_table

   WHERE column LIKE '_NNNN'

5. - SELECT FROM name_of_table

WHERE column LIKE '_NNNN_'

So, to summarize, it doesn't matter whether you put the underscore or percentage symbol on one side of the "NNNN" or on both, as long as they're present.

NNNN here can be any string or numerical value, and you can combine any N conditions by utilizing the OR and AND operators.

When it comes to the ORDER BY clause, that is usually utilized when you need to sort the data ascendingly or descendingly. This will be done by basing it off of 1-N columns. Keep in mind though, that some databases have an ORDER BY clause set as ascending by default.

When it comes to the syntax for the ORDER BY clause, it's a bit more complex than those we've looked at so far, so make sure to pay good attention to it. The syntax is:

SELECT list-column

FROM name_of_table

[WHERE your condition]

[ORDER BY column01, column02, .. column0N] [ASC | DESC];

Keep in mind you can use more than a single column with the ORDER BY clause. It's possible to manipulate and access any N columns at the same time. It's important to ascertain that whichever column you're currently sorting is the column that should be in the list-column.

Let us consider the previous customer example once again:

```
+--+----------+-----+-----------+----------+
| ID | NAME | AGE | ADDRESS  | SALARY  |
+--+----------+-----+-----------+----------+
| 1 | Ilija      | 19 | Tom_St  | 1500.00 |
| 2 | Frank    | 52 | Tom_St     | 1300.00 |
| 3 | Jim       | 53 | Tom_St     | 1200.00 |
| 4 | Martinia| 54 | Tom_St | 1900.00 |
| 5 | Jaffar   | 66 | Tom_St  | 1000.00 |
| 6 | Tim      | 33 | Tom_St     | 1000.00 |
| 7 | Kit       | 24 | Tom_st    | 1000.00 |
+--+----------+-----+-----------+----------+
```

You might want to sort your customers in ascending order by their names and salary. You might want to do this so you can know which ones pay the most and which pay the least, so you can later make informed decisions about this, you would do it as follows:

SQL> SELECT * FROM CUSTOMER

  ORDER BY NAME, SALARY;

If you did this, you would get a result where Jaffar is first, Jim 2nd and so on. Although it would also take salary into consideration, so the list may not be precisely as you would expect.

On the other hand, if you simply wanted to sort by name, that would look like:

SQL> SELECT * FROM CUSTOMER

  ORDER BY NAME;

The ORDER BY clause is extremely important to remember, as sorting and order play a heavy hand in many programs.

 TOP

The TOP clause in SQL does just what it says on the tin. It will output the top N or N percent of entries from a given table. This can make it useful when organizing data, as most of the time you won't need every single data point.

An important thing to notice here is that not all databases use the TOP clause. MySQL will use LIMIT in its place, doing functionally the same thing as a TOP clause does in regular SQL. Oracle also uses the ROWNUM command to do the exact same thing.

All in all, just remember to check which database you're using before using the TOP clause, as one of its relatives may be more appropriate.

The essential syntax for the TOP clause, with a necessary SELECT statement, is:

SELECT TOP number|percent name_of_column(s)

FROM name_of_table

WHERE [your_condition]

Returning back to the familiar customer example, here's how you would separate the top 3 from the following table:

```
+--+----------+-----+-----------+----------+
| ID | NAME     | AGE | ADDRESS   | SALARY   |
+--+----------+-----+-----------+----------+
```

1	Ilija	19	Uruguay	1500.00
2	Frank	52	France	200.00
3	Jim	53	Serbia	8040.00
4	Martinia	54	Amsterdam	9410.00
5	Jaffar	66	Podgorica	55200.00
6	Tim	33	Prune	1200.00
7	Kit	24	England	700.00

+--+----------+-----+----------+----------+

SQL> SELECT TOP 3 * FROM CUSTOMERS;

The output of this would be:

+--+----------+-----+----------+----------+

| ID | NAME | AGE | ADDRESS | SALARY |

+--+----------+-----+----------+----------+

1	Ilija	19	Urugu	1500.00
2	Frank	52	France	200.00
3	Jim	53	Serbia	8040.00

+--+----------+-----+----------+----------+

Now, the TOP clause isn't used very often in business. With that being said, it can sometimes be useful when it comes to mathematics and sciences. Many mathematical functions rely on finding the first X numbers of a sequence and doing something to them. You could separate these using a TOP clause with ease.

While it isn't the most useful clause, it is nonetheless necessary to learn in order to progress as an SQL developer.

Conclusion

With this, we have come to the end of this book. I thank you once again for choosing this book.

In today's world, there is a lot of data that is made available to you. If you own a business or want to start a business, you must know how to take care of the data you collect and use that information to improve the functioning of the business. You should also learn to store the information in one location, to ensure that you can access it whenever necessary. Whether you are trying to hold on to the personal information of your customers in one place or you are more interested in putting the sales information in an easy to look at way, you need to have a database that is easy to use.

In this guidebook, we are going to spend some time talking about SQL and how you can use it in a manner that will help you to deal with all your data management needs. SQL is a simple language that can help you analyze your data regardless of the type of business you run. We are going to cover some of the basic information you need to make this system work for you.

There is so much that you can learn about when it comes to SQL and using this system to make your business more successful. This guidebook is going to help you to get started so that you can organize and access your data any time you want to.

www.ingramcontent.com/pod-product-compliance
Lightning Source LLC
Chambersburg PA
CBHW052139070326
40690CB00047B/1192